BRITAIN AND THE WORLD

1. The Early Years

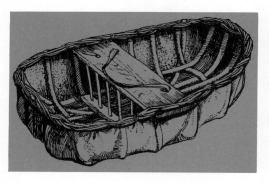

Illustrations by

TREVOR STUBLEY

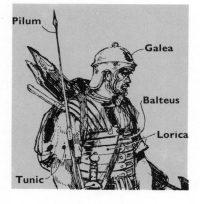

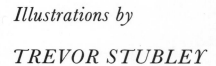

0 7217 1556 7

First printed 1970
Reprinted 1972

by C. Tinling & Co. Ltd,
Prescot

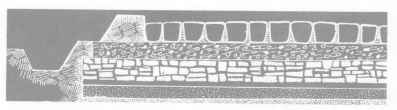

BRITAIN AND THE WORLD

The Early Years

By P. A. Darvill B.A., M.Litt. & W. R. Stirling M.A. (Cantab.)

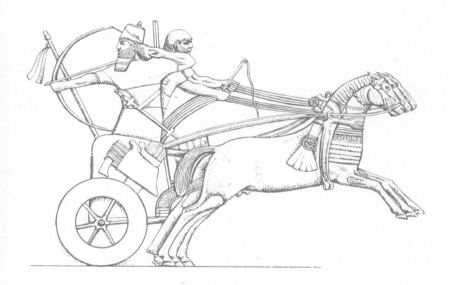

SCHOFIELD & SIMS LTD · HUDDERSFIELD

PREFACE

Each of the first four books in this series is divided into two parts: a chronological narrative and a collection of ten sections. The narrative aims to preserve the flow of history, whilst the sections give details of ten basic aspects of the life of mankind.

The narrative of each book is cross-referenced with the sections by a number of marginal notes. Thus a pupil can follow up in more detail many of the topics dealt with in the narrative.

With a collection of all four volumes to hand, a teacher has, apart from the narrative, a set of ten sections covering the span of time from prehistory to the twentieth century. Such a collection can form a good starting point for project work on topics such as farming, building or a particular industry. Each set of sections is a book within a series, whilst each volume in the series is a book within a book.

ACKNOWLEDGEMENTS

The authors and publishers wish to thank the following for permission to use copyright photographs:

South African Museum: p. 8.
Paul Popper Ltd.: pp. 11, 15, 19, 30, 36, 37, 45, 51, 60, 62, 65, 69, 71, 105 (2), 141, 142, 143, 146.
Ashmolean Museum: pp. 12 (2), 109, 141, 144.
The British Museum: pp. 13, 26, 27, 39, 85, 99, 142, 143 (2), 145, 149.
The Mansell Collection: pp. 23, 29, 37, 43, 52, 69, 73, 75.
Ministry of Public Building and Works: pp. 50, 70 (Crown Copyright).
Aerofilms Ltd.: pp. 59, 96.
The National Museum of Antiquities of Scotland: p. 81.
Ordnance Survey: p. 86 (Crown Copyright reserved).
J. K. St. Joseph, Cambridge University Collection: p. 88 (copyright reserved).
National Monuments Record: pp. 105, 146, 147.
Antony Miles Ltd., Salisbury: p. 107.
The National Museum, Copenhagen: p. 108.
The French Archaeological School of Athens: p. 144.
E.N.I.T., Rome: p. 145.
A. F. Kersting: p. 146.
Canon Maurice H. Ridgway, F.S.A., for permission to use the photograph by the late Fred H. Crossley: p. 147.
G. Bernard Wood: p. 147.
John Allegro: p. 158.

CONTENTS

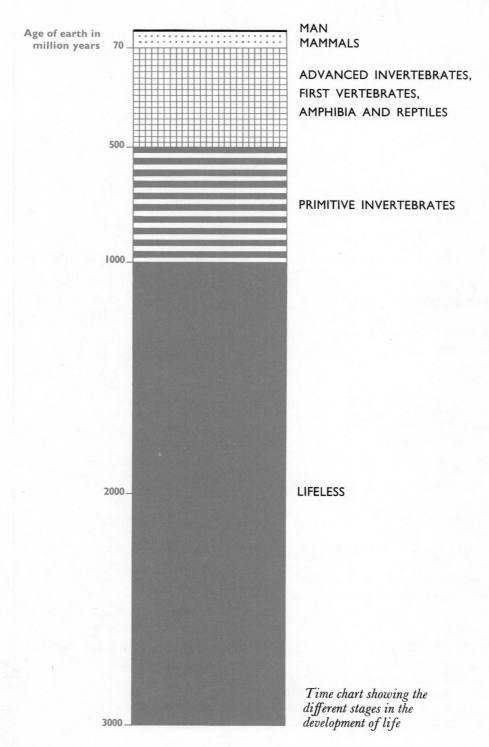

Age of earth in million years

70 — MAN
MAMMALS

ADVANCED INVERTEBRATES,
FIRST VERTEBRATES,
AMPHIBIA AND REPTILES

500 —

PRIMITIVE INVERTEBRATES

1000 —

2000 — LIFELESS

Time chart showing the different stages in the development of life

3000 —

Early Man

EARLY MAN

If we go backwards in time, the outline of man and his story becomes very faint. The earliest men on the earth had to achieve such feats as walking upright and speaking. If you have been in a zoo and have watched the monkeys grimace and listened to them chatter, then you were possibly seeing a living example of one stage in the way in which speech began. Men have developed from man-like apes, which in turn developed from other mammals, and in the diagram opposite an attempt has been made to show how short a time man has had to influence life on earth.

The Age of Man, the last 200 000 years, is so minute in comparison with the age of the Earth that it is represented on the diagram by a single line.

Some 10 000 or 15 000 years ago the people of the Old Stone Age lived on our earth. These were people who hunted or gathered their food. They had not learned to grow plants or keep animals. If we could be equipped with a time machine which could transport us back some 10 000 years we could learn a great deal about the life of men in those times. Since such machines do not exist, we shall have to use our imagination along with the evidence archaeologists have discovered.

Imagine waking early in the dark inner part of a cave; it is cold, for the fire near the cave mouth has gone out. The rest of the family might wake soon, so you hurry to the cave mouth to pick up whatever is left of the evening meal. You do not have much luck, for the meat which was left is being dried, to be eaten when food is scarce.

The day is to be spent hunting and everybody has a job to do, even the women and children. Near to the cave there

Bushman's Rock Painting from Africa

is a ravine with only one entrance. It can be used as a trap for animals. Yesterday the hunters saw a large herd of bison and today, with luck, we hope to drive them into the ravine so that some of them can be killed. The women and children, directed by two of the men, are given the task of driving the herd towards the ravine whilst the hunters gather large stones on the ledges at the top of the ravine. The stones will be levered down on to the bison when they are trapped below.

The herd is found, driven into the ravine, and soon the large stones hurtle through the air killing four bison. The remaining beasts are allowed to escape, for the four which have been killed will keep us in food for some time. Nothing is wasted. You can see, we are not wild, brutal savages, but a family working together to survive in a hard world.

The study of primitive people can help us to understand the habits of our Stone Age ancestors. Methods of making fire such as striking flint against iron, or using a fire drill have been used for centuries, and the latter was certainly used in Ancient Egypt. We can only guess how man came to make his first fires, and one possibility is that flint chipping, which was a common occupation, sometimes made sparks.

Once this discovery took place man's whole way of life changed. He could live in caves and wild animals could be kept at bay. He could cook his food. He could send signals by fire from hill to hill, and of course he had fire to give him light.

Making fire using firesticks

8

With fire, man could live in colder climates and he did not need to move to warmer places in winter. Lastly, fire enabled men to smelt ore, to hammer iron, and to develop such arts as glass-blowing.

Another tremendous discovery was that of language, but no one knows how it started. Things could be given names, memories could be used to make new ideas, discoveries and skills could be passed on to someone else, education became possible. If you have ever tried to make a foreigner understand you by using gestures, you will realise how difficult it was to communicate with someone else before speech developed.

The discovery of fire and the development of speech hastened the advance of primitive man and he became "a tool-making animal". You can follow the story of man's technical achievements in the sections at the back of this book, but remember that without fire and without language many of them might never have taken place.

The taming of animals and the growing of bread crops allowed men to become herdsmen or farmers. Herdsmen like Abraham and Jacob wandered from pasture to pasture with flocks of goats and sheep. Others became farmers, especially in such places as the Nile valley and the area of land between the rivers Tigris and Euphrates, where annual floods brought fresh soil. These floods, which deposited a layer of mud, made it unnecessary to move when the soil was exhausted. As primitive people had little idea of the need for manures, permanent settlement was difficult except in areas favoured by annual floods.

The early history of mankind is divided into ages which take their names from the main material used in the construction of tools or weapons. Thus we have the Stone Ages, the Bronze Age and the Iron Age. The changeover from stone to metal was gradual and although metals such as iron have obvious advantages over stone, stone tools must not be underrated.

In Denmark an interesting experiment took place which showed the usefulness of stone tools. A woodcutter using a stone axe cut down twenty-six pine trees, each of which was twenty centimetres in diameter. These logs were made into planks and timber for floor, roof and walls and after eighty-one days of hard work a timber house was built. This feat was carried out by one man with stone tools.

So far as we can judge a map of the world in 10 000 B.C. would be very similar in outline to the world of today. Generally it was a wetter and more fertile world.

Agriculture

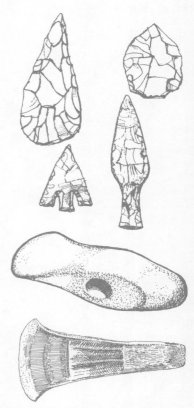

Stone Age and Bronze Age tools

9

MEDITERRANEAN SEA

Nile Delta

Rosetta
Alexandria
Sais
Tanis
Bubastis

Lower Kingdom

Giza
Heliopolis
Cairo
Memphis

Lake Mœris

Medinet el Faiyum

Herakleopolis

Gulf of Suez

Beni Hasan

Hermopolis

El Bersha
Akhetaten

NILE

Abydos
Dendera
Thebes
Karnak
Luxor

Hierakonpolis
Edfu

Elephantine
Philæ
Aswan
1st Cataract

Upper Kingdom

Fertile Areas

Abu Simbel

The Two Kingdoms of Upper and Lower Egypt

The First Civilisations

Egypt

The first civilisations appeared on the Eastern shores of the Mediterranean and in the Near East, and it is worth trying to recapture some of the excitement felt by the archaeologists who dug up the remains of the splendour of Ancient Egypt. Most of the tombs of the Pharaohs had been robbed, but by a strange accident the tomb of Tutankhamen was spared. The workers who tunnelled higher up the cliff where Tutankhamen was buried threw a great quantity of stone down and this covered the face of the tomb. The tomb remained undiscovered until 1922. The pictures show you some of the objects found in the tomb.

The map shows you the two kingdoms of Upper and Lower Egypt, the earliest known nations in the world. Each kingdom had a capital and the people lived in villages along the side of the Nile. About the forty-third century B.C. a powerful king of Lower Egypt marched from the Delta into Upper Egypt, conquered it and united the two kingdoms. In this new kingdom the first civilisation developed.

10

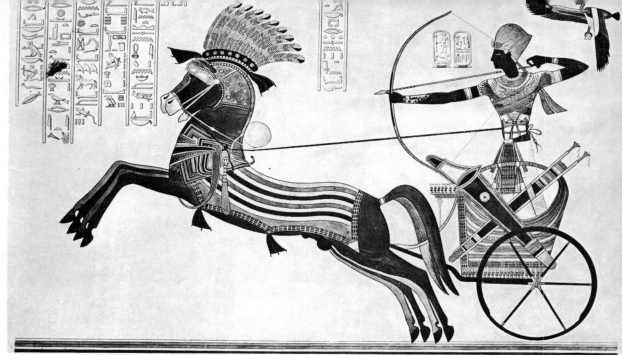

Sesostris, a legendary king of Egypt

Religion, government and the calendar show how dependent the Egyptians were on the river Nile. The river, the earth and the plants were represented by Osiris, the god of imperishable life.

Government

One of the main tasks of the king was to organise the irrigation system, and to do this well he needed a calendar. The Egyptian calendar was divided into three seasons, the flood, the coming forth of the crops, and the harvest.

Agriculture

Later, the time between floods was calculated to be three hundred and sixty-five days, which was divided into twelve (moon) months of thirty days each, the remaining five days, sensibly enough, were used for feasting.

Ideas

Sumer

The first civilisations appeared in the fertile valleys of the rivers Tigris and Euphrates about 4000 B.C. Wheat, barley and meat were plentiful in this area, and there was no need for man to move from land that was exhausted. Cities with several thousands of inhabitants grew up; these needed considerable organisation. Writing was invented, and this was very important in a land where a record of property had to be kept. It is from writing that we get history, and an early example of picture writing is shown in the illustration above.

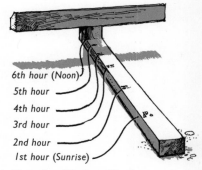

6th hour (Noon)
5th hour
4th hour
3rd hour
2nd hour
1st hour (Sunrise)

Egyptian Shadow Clock

11

The head of Tutankhamen

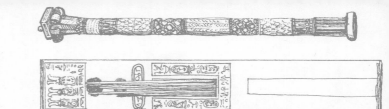

A scribe's palette and case for writing reeds

A papyrus smoother

Building

The largest buildings found in these cities were the temples or ziggurats. The priests were powerful and accepted tribute from the people to please the gods. The white temple of Uruk was dedicated to the sky god Anu and was built about 3200 B.C.

In Babylon in the reign of King Hammurabi (1728–1686 B.C.) clay tablets were used for keeping records and we can well imagine the scene when King Hammurabi dictated a letter to one of his secretaries. The king would give orders in brief, clear sentences to his secretary who would take his reed stylus from a leather holder at his girdle, and would cover the clay tablet with groups of wedge-shaped lines. When the king had finished, the secretary would sprinkle some dry, powdered clay over the wet tablet to prevent it sticking to the envelope. A clay

Hammurabi dictating to a secretary

envelope was then drawn over the tablet and sent to the furnace to be baked. Many of these clay tablets are still in existence and contain details of the day to day work of this king.

The work of the Egyptian postman would be lighter than that of one in Babylon, for the Egyptians used split papyrus reed as paper, a pointed reed as a pen and an ink made from a mixture of water, gum and soot. Paper, pen and ink have descended to us from the Egyptians who also produced the first alphabet.

The discoveries made by the Egyptians and other peoples in the Eastern Mediterranean, Asia Minor and Mesopotamia were not always put to peaceful uses and between the fifteenth century B.C. and the fifth century B.C. one nation after another established its rule over other peoples.

The Assyrians

Perhaps the most terrible of the conquering nations were the Assyrians. The city kingdom of Assur (see page 14) was often attacked, from both the north and south and to survive it had to have a large, efficient army.

The Assyrians were some of the first people to use horses and chariots in their armies. They also developed colossal battering rams which could demolish the sun-dried brick walls of the cities they attacked. The Assyrian kings, Sargon II (722–705 B.C.) and Sennacherib (705–681 B.C.), and later Nebuchadnezzar the Chaldean were powerful rulers who had magnificent palaces.

Clay tablet with Cuneiform writing

The Art of War

An Assyrian battering ram

The Hanging Gardens of Babylon in Nebuchadnezzar's palace were one of the wonders of the world. The trees were planted in a deep layer of earth which was on top of a waterproofed arched cellar. Gardens surrounded the central rooms where officials worked in the cool shade, a pleasure enjoyed by few, even in modern cities.

The Chaldean priests made a thorough study of the heavens and they thought that the five planets Mercury, Venus, Mars, Jupiter and Saturn controlled the fortunes of men. These planets, together with the sun and the moon, were each worshipped once a week, and in time the name of the god worshipped was given to the day itself. Since our language came to us via the Scandinavian lands there are Norse words in it such as Woden's day or Wednesday. The Chaldean origin of Sun-day, Moon-day and Saturn-day is clear enough.

Persia

The Persians were the next people to establish an empire by conquest and soon it extended from Egypt to India. The earlier Persian rulers were skilful and efficient, but later rulers were shown to be cruel tyrants by the Greeks, who after three wars drove them from Europe. Before we deal with these wars we must trace the early history of the Greeks and say something of the career of Heinrich Schliemann.

The World as seen by Herodotus, a Greek historian

The Ancient World

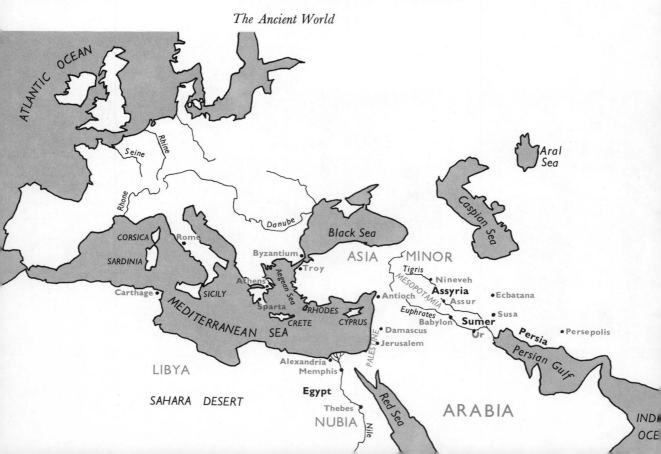

Minoan bull leaping sport

Crete

One thing that is difficult to realise is that the history of mankind is not a story of continual progress. Often people in one country, such as the Cretans of 1600–1400 B.C., reached a high standard of civilisation which, when lost, was hardly reached again by them. The picture shows you the throne room of the palace of Knossos, whilst the one above shows a sport which few of us would like to try. The palace had running water and bathrooms. Women's clothing included flounced dresses and corsets. About 1400 B.C. disaster hit Knossos and the palace was destroyed, never to be rebuilt.

Greece

The first Greek civilisation grew up on the Greek mainland between 1400 and 1200 B.C., but after this time there was a Dark Age. Much of our information about these early Greeks comes from either archaeologists, or the epic poems of Homer. People still argue about the writer of these poems, some saying they were the work of the blind poet Homer, others saying they must be the work of many men. The Greeks had singers and reciters who performed the epics, the "Iliad" and the "Odyssey", and so the poems were passed on by word of mouth.

Hundreds of years later in January 1830 we could have seen a seven year old boy, Heinrich Schliemann, sitting at home reading the book his father gave him for Christmas. It was "Jerrer's Universal History", a book almost as heavy as young Heinrich. One picture showed the burning of Troy, and even at

The throne at Knossos

15

Greek City States

Transport by Sea

Government

the age of seven this boy was eager to see if the walls of Troy mentioned in this legend still remained. Very often we forget the ambitions of childhood, but Heinrich Schliemann did not, and as soon as he had become a successful business man he set about planning to dig up the ruins of Troy. This seemed a crazy scheme for Troy had disappeared and to many was no more than a legend, but Schliemann found the ruins of this city and a considerable number of gold ornaments. He had used Homer's writings as his guide and a legend had become a fact.

Greece was and still is a mountainous country with a very jagged coastline. This made travel overland very difficult, so the best means of transport was by sea-going ships. For this reason many cities were built near to or on the coast. The city states governed themselves, and each was made up of the city and land outside it where crops such as wheat, vines and olives were grown. Athens, the largest city state, was as big as Derbyshire, about 2500 square kilometres in area.

Only citizens took an active part in the government of Athens. In 431 B.C. they numbered about 40 000. The citizens met regularly and this form of government in which the people play an active part was, and still is, called democracy.

The Greeks never became one nation, they remained city states, some of the most important being Athens, Sparta, Thebes (not to be confused with the Egyptian city of the same name), Corinth and Argos.

An Athenian Boy and a Spartan Boy

A description of the upbringing of an Athenian boy and a Spartan boy will give you some idea of the difference between life in these two cities. If an Athenian boy were to have written an account of his life between his birth and the time when he became a citizen it might well have run like this:

"After I had been born my father put a wreath of olive leaves outside our house of sun-baked brick to tell our neighbours and friends that the birth of a son had taken place. Five days after my birth my father took off his cloak and took me in his arms and ran swiftly around the hearth. He did this so that the hearth gods would look after me when I was learning to walk and make me steady and fleet-footed. On the tenth day I was given a name and a feast was held in my honour.

16

A piece of pottery showing an Athenian Grammar School

After this I was put in the care of a nurse, the most trusted woman slave who worked for our family. My food consisted of broth, barley porridge and cheese and afterwards I was given the sweet scented honey collected from the bees which fed on the hills around Athens. I was told the stories of the great heroes such as Hector and Achilles and often played with my earthenware rattle and model soldiers made from clay or lead.

When I was seven I was put in the charge of a pedagogue, who took me to school and brought me home when lessons were finished. He made sure I was well-mannered and beat me if I disobeyed. Our school was near to the coast and after a wrestling bout we bathed in the sea. We had to keep fit, and running, jumping and throwing spears were part of our education. Our minds were trained as well as our bodies and reading, writing, arithmetic, drawing and music were the main subjects we studied. We wrote with a stylus on wax and a few of us were allowed to use Egyptian papyrus and a pen.

By the age of fourteen I could play the double pipe and the lyre very well and I looked forward to performing in public one day. At sixteen I had my hair cut short for this was the age when I began my military training and played my part in manning the defences of my city. Having completed this service I could become a citizen and play my part in governing my city."

Agriculture

Lyre

Double pipe

B

17

In Sparta things were different for even at birth the Spartan family was loyal to the city's belief in a military upbringing. If the child looked too weak to become a soldier it was left out in the mountains to die. At seven, a boy was taken away from home and brought up at a military school. Here the boys were strictly disciplined and made to bear hardship. They were given tasks which included stealing and the only reason for a boy being in disgrace was his failure. There is one story of a Spartan boy who brought back a young fox under his tunic. In attempting to get free the fox bit the boy, but rather than complain the boy let the fox bite him to death. The older boys sometimes acted as spies on the helots or slaves, and attempted to find out leaders who might stir up rebellion. Any so found would be killed.

On one occasion in 424 B.C. the Spartans, afraid that the Athenians would stir up a rising among the helots, sent round a proclamation asking the helots to choose from among themselves those who were bravest in facing the enemy. Two thousand were selected. These the Spartans guessed would be good leaders if the helots revolted, so to prevent any chance of revolt they murdered them.

When the Spartan boy was fully trained as a soldier he was willing to obey any order. His mother bade him farewell in the Spartan manner. She handed him his shield and said "Come back with this or on it."

The Persian War

The threat of the Persian Empire to the Greek mainland led to the Greek cities helping one another, but after the final defeat of the Persians it was not long before they went their own independent ways once more.

The first Persian invasion of Greece itself followed the victory by Persia over the rebellious Greek cities on the Asian coast. Darius the Persian king did not forget the help sent by the Athenians to the Greeks in Asia, and decided to send a fleet to attack Athens. This fleet was wrecked off Mount Athos in 492 B.C. Two years later the Persians sent heralds to ask all the Greek cities to submit; many did, but Athens and Sparta refused.

Darius decided to use force and a fleet was once more sent to attack Athens. This fleet took a different route from the first one and the army was landed north of Athens at the bay of Marathon.

The Athenians sent a runner to Sparta with a request for

Persian bowman

18

The Plain of Marathon

help. He took only two days to cover the 160 kilometres between the cities. The Spartans refused to march until the moon was full as this marked the end of certain religious ceremonies, so the Athenians were left to meet the Persians without their help.

The Athenians took up a position overlooking the main road to Athens, and after unsuccessful attempts to lure them from their position the Persians marched along the road. The Athenians had to face the Persian bowmen, but they did not falter, and as soon as the wings of the Athenian army got to close quarters their spears spread havoc among the enemy. The Persians fled for their ships, leaving 6000 dead on the Plain of Marathon.

The Art of War

The Persian Wars

A Persian galley

Although the Persian fleet appeared off Athens no troops were landed and they sailed away. It was clear that the Persians would attack again, although Darius their king died soon after the repulse of the second invasion.

Next, his son Xerxes gathered a war fleet together and the Greek historian Herodotus describes how a bridge of boats was constructed across the Hellespont so that the Persian army could march into Greece. Whilst the army marched by land the fleet followed by sea. In this third invasion the Athenians did get help from the Spartans, and Leonidas, the Spartan leader and his army were wiped out in their gallant defence of the pass of Thermopylae.

This battle was one of the great delaying actions of history. The Greeks held up the Persian army for several days in the summer of 480 B.C. and were only outflanked by the treachery of a Greek who told the Persians of a secret track which led to the other end of the pass.

After their victory at Thermopylae, the Persians marched on Athens. The Athenian statesman Themistocles had made sure that the people of Athens had been ferried to the little island of Salamis before the Persians arrived. Imagine what it was like watching Athens burn from one of the islands, and knowing that the Persian host was camped in your city.

Themistocles did not despair and drew Xerxes to attack by sending a false message which told of the Greek fleet preparing to escape from the bay. Xerxes, keen to wipe out the Greeks, decided to order the attack and to watch the final destruction of his enemies from his throne on the shore. Xerxes' fleet was large, but in the confined space of the bay the Greeks had the advantage for they could manoeuvre much better than their opponents. The battle lasted a whole day and by sunset the Persian fleet had been destroyed. The powerful Athenian fleet had saved Greece. The Persian army suffered defeat at Plataea in 479 B.C., and so the third attempt to conquer Greece failed.

Building

The Athenians rebuilt their city in marble, which was the best material they had. One new building was the Parthenon. It topped the hill, called the Acropolis, and shows us the greatness of Athens in the fifth century B.C. You can build up a fuller picture of the other features of Greek life by using the sections at the end of this book.

The Arts

Ideas

The other city states were jealous of Athens. They hated its prosperity and resented paying their share towards the cost of the combined fleet. War broke out, and led by Sparta the

20

other cities eventually defeated Athens. The war lasted thirty years, from 435 to 404 B.C.

Philip of Macedon

North of the Greek states lay Macedonia where Philip of Macedon ruled from 360 B.C. onwards. Philip had had a Greek education and loved the Greek way of life. He was very shrewd. He realised that the city states were exhausted and planned to make himself master of all Greece. He based his policy on a strong army, and his infantry and cavalry were some of the best in the Ancient World.

The Art of War

Like any skilled and crafty ruler he got as much as he could without fighting. His skill was noticed by the Athenian Demosthenes who spoke of the danger of Philip to the Athenian Assembly. Despite his warnings the Greeks were defeated and Philip became ruler of all the Greek states except Sparta, the last to hold out.

Philip was stabbed by a noble during the revelries at the wedding of his daughter in 336 B.C. and his kingdom passed to his son, Alexander.

Alexander The Great

Philip had taken particular care with his son's education. He appointed Aristotle, the greatest philosopher of that time, as the boy's tutor and Philip shared his own ideas with Alexander as well. At eighteen Alexander was given charge of the cavalry, and even though he was only twenty when his father was murdered, Alexander was prepared for ruling Macedonia and his father's conquests. He had two aims; to establish his rule, then to add to his father's conquests.

Ideas

The death of a conqueror is often a sign for the beaten to revolt, and the city of Thebes took what was thought to be a good opportunity to shake off Macedonian rule. Alexander marched swiftly southward through the pass of Thermopylae and was soon at the gates of Thebes. The city was destroyed except for the house of Pindar, a Greek poet of earlier times. Alexander left it standing to show that although he would stamp out rebellion he would respect Greek learning. He was a conqueror, of this there is no doubt, but he was not a tyrant destroying all signs of civilisation.

In 334 B.C. Alexander crossed into Asia to attack Persia and to bring most of the known world under his rule. He never returned to Greece and it was fortunate for him that his father had had in his court men of great ability and loyalty who were able to govern in Alexander's absence.

Aristotle

21

Map labels: BLACK SEA · Troy · Battle of Granicus 334 B.C. · Gordium (The Gordian knot) · CASPIAN SEA · Sardis · Athens · Sparta · Cilician Gap · Battle of Issus · Arbela · Battle of Gaugamela · MEDITERRANEAN SEA · Euphrates · Tigris · Ecbatana · Alexandria · Damascus · Siege of Tyre 332 B.C. · Babylon (Alexander died) · Susa · Jerusalem · Memphis · Persepolis (Xerxes' palace burnt) · PERSIAN GULF · 100 200 300 400 500 600 700 800 Kilometres · 100 200 300 400 500 Miles · Nile · RED SEA · Alexander's route

Alexander's Conquests

The Art of War

The first important battle he won against the Persians was near the river Granicus and after the victory he marched to the temple of Gordium. Here he was shown a chariot which had its yoke attached to the pole by a complicated knot. It was said that whoever untied the knot would rule the world. Alexander could not untie the knot with his fingers, so he cut it with his sword. We use the phrase "cutting the Gordian knot" to mean that a forceful direct way has been found to solve a problem.

At the battle of Issus in 333 B.C. the Persian king Darius III fought against Alexander, and lost. Two years later Alexander fought his greatest battle at Gaugamela and Darius asked for terms. Many of Alexander's councillors urged him to call a halt to his conquests now that his father's aims had been achieved. Alexander decided to continue despite their counsel, and after the battle of Arbela learned that Darius had been murdered by some of his own treacherous attendants. Alexander made sure the body was returned to the Persian royal family to whom he gave protection and hospitality.

After the complete conquest of Persia he marched eastward into Afghanistan and into India through the valley of Kabul. Hercules, whom Alexander claimed as an ancestor, was said to have fought in this part of India. The campaign in India lasted two years but nearly brought disaster, for his soldiers were exhausted, homesick and close to mutiny.

On the way back Alexander made his epic journey down the River Indus to the Indian Ocean. The Macedonians knew nothing of tides for there were no real tides in the Mediterranean. Thus it came as a great shock when ships left safely at

22

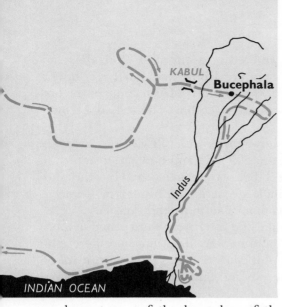

Alexander the Great

anchor at one of the branches of the Indus delta were left high and dry, to be refloated some hours later and damaged by the rapid incoming tide. Alexander made prompt sacrifices on an island near the mouth of the Indus.

Later he gave his admiral Nearchus the task of exploring the sea which lay between the mouth of the Indus and the Persian Gulf. Alexander marched back with his army by the land route. When he met Nearchus again the admiral was unwashed, pale and with such long hair that he was scarcely recognisable. However, the fleet was safe and Nearchus had carried out a successful exploration.

In his earlier campaign in Egypt in 331 B.C. Alexander had mixed war and exploration and had set up the city of Alexandria. It grew to be a centre of learning after his death in 323 B.C.

His eagerness to inquire into all branches of learning and to spread Greek ideas had a profound effect on the empire he ruled. He sought to win the approval of his subjects not only by wearing the clothes of a Persian king, but by encouraging his officers to marry Persian and Babylonian women. Alexander seemed to be a superman to many people and he was worshipped as a god. The Egyptians thought he was the child of the sun god. Tales of his victories have been passed down through the centuries, but they are not as important as his search for knowledge. He sent expeditions to find the reason for the annual overflow of the Nile, and another to circumnavigate the Caspian Sea. It is for these ventures as much as his remarkable series of conquests that he should be remembered to-day.

23

Rome

So far Italy has not entered into our story, but after the break-up of Alexander's empire Rome and Carthage fought for control of the trade of the Western Mediterranean. Before we study these wars we must trace how Rome had become important.

The legends describe how Tarquin the Proud, the last king of Rome, was driven out in 509 B.C., and how on his return a wooden bridge over the Tiber was defended by Horatius and his two friends. This single event in the history of Rome is typical of the way the Romans had to defend their city.

Rome became a republic and its citizens were proud of their city. Their outstanding qualities were discipline and thoroughness. Later, whilst Philip of Macedon was gaining control of Greece the Romans were gaining control of Italy. The Romans suffered many setbacks, but they learned from their defeats, and improved their army. Those who came under Roman rule gained the benefits of Roman life, and we shall see from the history of the Roman occupation of Britain that the benefits were immense.

By about 250 B.C. the Romans had gained control of Italy. Before this date the people of Messina in Sicily had appealed to the Romans to send help against the Carthaginians. As a result the Romans decided to wage war against Carthage and

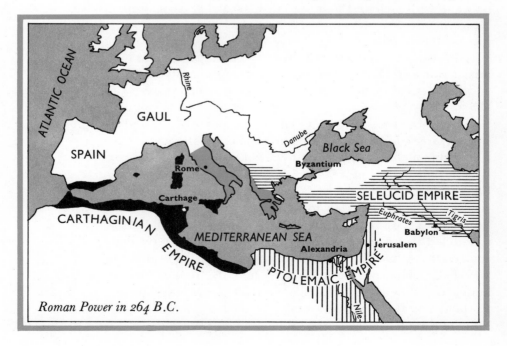

Roman Power in 264 B.C.

24

in 264 B.C. the first of the three wars between Rome and Carthage began.

The Romans built a large fleet, and although not experienced in sea warfare they had one surprise for their opponents. They devised a way of making fighting at sea as much like a land battle as possible. They invented the corvus, a wooden bridge with a spike on the end which was carried upright near the mast of the ship. When the Roman ship was close enough, the corvus was dropped on to the deck of the enemy ship, grappling the two ships together. Then the Romans boarded the enemy ship and used their opponents' deck as a battle field.

The war against Carthage lasted until 241 B.C. when, after many setbacks, the Romans defeated the Carthaginian fleet and prevented them from sending reinforcements to Sicily where the war had begun. The Romans imposed a hard peace on the Carthaginians, making them pay a huge sum of money for war damages. Rome took Sicily and the neighbouring islands, and later took Sardinia and Corsica.

Look at the map and you will see that Rome had now three very useful island outposts which could be used against Carthage. To counter this threat the Carthaginians under Hamilcar decided to invade Spain and their scheme was aided when fighting broke out between the Romans and the Gauls in Northern Italy.

The Corvus

Roman Power in 44 B.C.

25

*One side of a Coin
showing Hannibal*

Hannibal

Hamilcar died before he could invade Spain. His son Hannibal, who was only twenty-four, now took control of the Carthaginian army. There were several good reasons why Hannibal thought that the overland route through Spain into Northern Italy was a sound scheme. Firstly, his fleet was not strong enough to guard the transports he would require to carry his large army from Carthage to Southern Italy. Secondly, if he invaded Italy from the north he would be moving through land only recently taken from the Gauls by the Romans. The Gauls would surely help him in his invasion to get their own back on the Romans. Lastly, and possibly most important, an attack from the north which involved crossing the Alps would be unthinkable to many Romans, so it would take them by surprise if Hannibal succeeded.

Hannibal had another surprise for his enemies, for included in his army was a force of thirty-seven elephants. Some writers have refused to believe that a clever general like Hannibal would risk taking such large beasts on such a difficult route. Let us try to reconstruct his journey.

Hannibal and a large army landed in Spain and keeping close to the coast moved into Gaul and eventually reached the river Rhône. Sir Gavin de Beer, the famous historian, argues that they crossed the Rhône south of Arles where the river is widest and also slow and shallow. This would be a likely place to get the elephants across and there is a description of how this was done. The massive beasts refused to enter the boats and so a pier was built which jutted out into the river. The sides were banked up with earth and a raft, made to look like the end of the pier, was anchored to it. The elephants were led along the pier on to the raft and floated into midstream before they realised what had been done. Some panicked and were upset into the water, but they were near enough to the shore to wade across to dry land.

The next obstacle after crossing the Rhône was the Alps. The story of this climb may seem unbelievable, but during the Second World War, 1939–45, a band of elephants was marched by "Elephant Bill" from Burma over the mountains into India, and no one was more astonished than the planter who was the first to be told that the elephants on his plantation had escaped from the Japanese. Hannibal's difficulties were increased by trouble with the Gauls who were not so friendly as he had hoped. Treacherous guides misled him and caused his army to suffer unnecessary casualties.

26

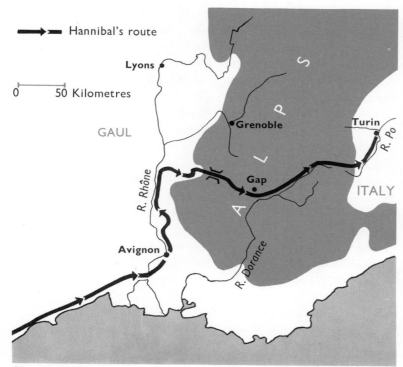

The other side of the coin showing an elephant

Hannibal's Route

Hannibal took a high and dangerous pass through the Alps and lost a number of animals and men. At one point rock had to be cracked so that it could be moved from their way. This was done by lighting a fire on the rock and then drenching it with vinegar which, incidentally, was the strongest acid known to people at this time. It was the sudden change in temperature which caused the rock to break.

By the spring of 217 B.C. Hannibal and his army had descended to the valley of the river Po and their victories encouraged many Gauls to join them. Soon he was within striking distance of Rome, but did not attack for he had no siege machines, and he felt he did not have enough men. He marched eastward, collected more horses and provisions, and was then ready to meet the Roman army.

The Romans appointed Fabius as dictator. His scheme was to wear Hannibal out by refusing to give battle and by harassing his forces. Hannibal did meet the Roman army on four occasions during his first two years in Italy and won each time. His greatest victory was at Cannae where a Roman army was almost completely wiped out. Roman leaders wore rings as an indication of their rank, and it is said that after this battle

27

Hannibal sent hundreds of these rings back to Carthage.

Rome did not yield, and slaves and boys were pressed into the army and gradually the Romans recovered. Once more Hannibal marched to Rome, this time to the gates. Ten years in Italy and Rome had not fallen, so Hannibal sent for his brother Hasdrubal and a relief army. This army was defeated before it could reach Hannibal and Hasdrubal was slain.

Now Rome had a run of victories, and under the leadership of Scipio drove the Carthaginians out of Italy. At Zama in North Africa, near to Carthage, Scipio defeated Hannibal. The Romans had won the second war and insisted that Hannibal, now a man of fifty, be sent into exile. Hannibal was hounded from one country to another and in the end poisoned himself.

The city of Carthage was destroyed in the third war between these two states and the Roman writer Polybius who stood by Scipio while it burned wrote, "It is glorious but, I know not how, I am somehow afraid, and I have a foreboding that another hereafter may give the same order about my city".

If the two maps on pages 24 and 25 are compared you can see how much more land the Romans had conquered between 264 B.C. and the death of Caesar in 44 B.C. The Romans during this time extended their control from Italy to almost all of the Mediterranean world.

Life in Rome

Trade

Rome's trade increased, new goods were in her markets, and new wealth flowed into the city. Let us see if life in Rome changed much.

Building

The single room house of an earlier period, made of sun-dried brick with a square hole in the middle of the roof would be smoky and dirty and beds, tables, pots and kettles would be in full view. These houses had nothing but the bare necessities in them and the Carthaginian ambassador was amused to see the same silver dishes at two dinners he attended. He guessed correctly that they had been loaned from one house to another.

Livy, the Roman historian, in describing the winter of 218–217 B.C. mentions that an ox escaped from the cattle market and went up the stairs of a house by the river. It jumped from the third storey of this house to the horror of the onlookers in the street. Rome, like any other rapidly developing city, had to build upwards. This brief description tells us that there was in Rome the ancient counterpart of the blocks of flats found in present-day cities.

28

The Ruins of the Trajan Forum, Rome

Transport was so slow that people could not travel to work from the outskirts—as so many do in large, modern, cities. They had to live in the city itself.

These city houses divided into apartments may have seemed imposing from the outside, but Roman writers have left us in no doubt about their shortcomings. The ground floor was the best to have, for it was probably better heated and was the only floor which could get a regular supply of water. Those who lived on the upper floors would have to go to the fountains for their water supply. Often these large tenements were badly built and some of them collapsed, but from the outside, tiles and mosaics made them attractive. But no amount of decoration can make up for insufficient light and heat and lack of sanitation.

Often people get a false impression of life in Rome, picturing the average Roman snug in his centrally-heated house, with beautiful mosaic floors, piped water supply and a water closet. The truth is that the furnaces were never used to heat a whole building. Generally just a section of, or even just one room, in a house was heated. The tenements did not have fireplaces so it is likely the inhabitants had to warm themselves by charcoal braziers.

29

The Pont du Gard, Nîmes

The great aqueducts brought a regular supply of water to Rome, but little of this went to private houses. Consequently, human water carriers were common in Rome even though one Roman estimated nearly 1000 million litres of water were brought by aqueduct each day. The system of sewers was good, but scarcely any private houses emptied their sewage into them. Glass was not used and either wooden shutters, cloth or skins were used to cover the window spaces.

If this picture seems sombre, it is partly offset by the fine public buildings in Rome.

Government   If we return to the first century B.C. and see how Rome was governed we find it still a republic, but very different from a modern European republic where all adults have the right to vote. When Rome was no more than a city of fifty square kilometres it could be governed as Athens had been in its heyday. Then the citizens of Rome at the blast of the horn from the Capitol would gather in the Popular Assembly. Here they would play their part in government with the patricians or noblemen who sat in the Senate, the other government body.

30

A Shaduf

The Senate was in some ways like the British House of Lords. But unlike the House of Commons, the Popular Assembly became weaker instead of stronger as the years went by. By the end of the wars against Carthage the Popular Assembly was made up of the riff-raff of Rome and a few unprincipled politicians. Roman citizenship was given to people of conquered races and so, at least in theory, all races of people could have crowded into the Popular Assembly at the sound of the horn from the Capitol. Many people had no money and no vote. This soon led to a dangerous situation.

In 73 B.C. the slaves revolted under the leadership of Spartacus the gladiator. For two years these men held out in the crater of Mount Vesuvius which seems to have been dormant in those days. The revolt failed and six thousand followers of Spartacus were crucified on the Appian Way, a grim reminder to the common people of what might happen to them in the event of another revolt. Rome was a republic in name only, for when government is weak people often put their trust in a strong man. Unfortunately such men are often selfish and ambitious. The period between 90 B.C. and 30 B.C. is known as the Age of Generals, and the greatest of these was Julius Caesar.

31

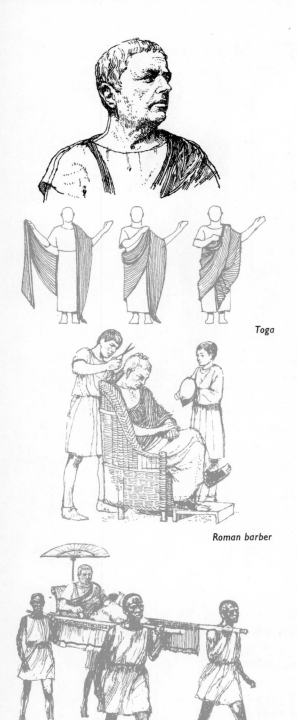

Toga

Roman barber

A Litter

A day in the Life of a Rich Roman Citizen and his Wife

The Husband's Day

Hora Prima
(first hour of day) 4.27–5.42 a.m. Awoke to the sound of the servants cleaning the house. Got up and dressed, with the aid of my wife who arranged my toga.

Hora Secunda
(second hour of day) 5.42–6.58 a.m. Had my breakfast, which was a cup of water. Did not wash, for I shall bathe this afternoon.

Hora Tertia
(third hour of day) 6.58–8.13 a.m. Called my barber who is going to curl my hair in the manner of the Emperor Hadrian. Decided to have the flaws in my complexion covered by patches which my barber has cunningly made. Only had my cheek cut once to-day, a record!

Hora Quarta
(fourth hour) 8.13–9.29 a.m. Late this morning at the warehouse. Would have been even later if my litter had not followed a legion leaving the city.

Hora Quinta
(fifth hour) 9.29–10.44 a.m. All the recent deliveries of goods had been checked when I arrived so I was able to see the surveyor in charge of the road widening scheme at the entrance to our building. It must be pleasant on a warm day to use one's groma to stake out the course of a new road.

Hora Sexta
(sixth hour) 10.44–12 noon. Spent a weary hour with some of our waggoners and muleteers trying to get them to speed up so that transport would not be so expensive.

32

The Wife's Day

Tire woman

Pin, brooch and comb

Roman kitchen

Hora Prima

Awakened by the noise made by my husband scolding the slaves for waking him up. Hurried to my husband to help him arrange his toga.

Hora Secunda

Sent for my tire woman to dress my hair. If my husband realised the time and skill it took to prepare my hair he would not talk of my hair towering above me. After chalking my brow and arms to make them beautifully white, my cheeks were ochred and my eyes made up with powdered antimony.

Hora Tertia

Chose my jewels for the day. Diadem for my hair, ear-rings, trinkets for my neck, bracelets, rings and circlets for my ankles. I did not forget my fan of peacock's feathers which is so useful in hot weather.

Hora Quarta

Busied myself instructing the staff in the work they have to do.

Hora Quinta

Instructed my servant to bring an umbrella and my mappa for I was intent on visiting my friend Volumnia.

Hora Sexta

As usual Volumnia insisted that we take something to eat at noon. We had some cold meat, vegetables and fruits washed down with some wine. I always tell her that patricians such as she should not do as the plebeians and take food at noon.

C

33

Four-wheeled waggon

Dining room

Stylus and writing tablet

Note
The length of "the hours" are at the summer solstice, about June 23rd, when the hours of the daylight are at their maximum. The length of the Roman hours were elastic, the twelve hours of the day being the time between sunrise and sunset. Clearly in winter these hours would be short in the summer they would be long.

The Husband's Day (*continued*)

Hora Septima
(seventh hour) 12.00–1.15 p.m. Took some time off for a meal then decided to check remaining goods from Spain, before leaving for a game of backgammon.

Hora Octava
(eighth hour) 1.15–2.31 p.m. Played and lost and decided to go to the baths before returning home for dinner.

Hora Nona
(ninth hour) 2.31–3.46 p.m. Returned home and soon we were lying on our divans awaiting dinner. Our children sat in front of us on stools. Our servants brought in the knives, spoons and tooth-picks and the ewers of perfumed water which we use to wash our hands after each course. We began with hors d'œuvres and a supply of hot rolls which were delicious. The Marseilles wine was unusually good. We followed this with pork from Gaul and a splendid selection of vegetables which the children enjoyed. The asparagus was especially good. The selection of fruit, pears, figs, pomegranates and dates was fine and the children gorged themselves on the pomegranates which had come from Africa in one of our own ships.

Hora Decima
(tenth hour) 3.46–5.02 p.m. By the end of this hour we had finished dinner and listened to what Lucius our son had to say about his first visit to the circus.

Hora Undecima
(eleventh hour) 5.02–6.17 p.m. Sat at my marble writing desk and after getting a new stylus and writing tablet, wrote an account of the day.

Hora Duodecima
(twelfth hour) 6.17–7.33 p.m. Prepared to go to bed.

34

The Wife's Day (*continued*)

Roman butcher

Hora Septima

We hired a litter and were taken to the baths where we intended to stay until the eighth hour when we would return for dinner. We went to the baths of Caracalla where there were shops, gardens and libraries.

Hora Octava

We were refreshed by the visit to the baths and returned to my house to see that dinner was being prepared.

Hora Nona

Everything ready for the return of my husband who, judging by his long face, had lost at backgammon. The dinner, unlike the banquets at some nearby houses where such dishes as dormice rolled in honey are served, is simple and nourishing. I should hate the children to grow up gluttons so we do not go in for the colossal meals some people have.

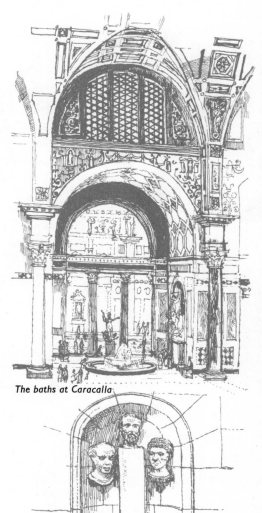

The baths at Caracalla

Hora Decima

Instructed the servants to clear up all the dishes.

Hora Undecima

After Lucius had told us about the circus I told him about our family and the virtues of his ancestors. I hope this will make him realise the importance of the wax masks of the most honourable members of our family which are in the recess in the central hall.

Hora Duodecima

Prepared to go to bed after joining my husband and family in prayer before the wax busts of our ancestors.

Masks

Julius Caesar

Pompey

Julius Caesar

Caesar is important not because he carried out two brief armed surveys of South-East England in 55 B.C. and 54 B.C. but because of what he did in Rome. His campaigns in Britain were to him nothing more than exploration and good publicity, for Roman generals often had political ambitions too. Caesar was a very efficient soldier, but he could be a ruthless one and his campaign in Gaul included the massacre of all the inhabitants of Bourges. His conquest of Gaul was successful and brutal, but he soon learned that to spare some opponents was a way of winning popularity.

He had been made a consul in 59 B.C. His greatest rival was Pompey, another great general. But Pompey was not so skilled a statesman as Caesar. When Caesar's second term as governor of Gaul neared its end the Senate, fearing his re-election as consul, summoned him to disband his army.

The popularity of Caesar was so great, and his ambitions so high, that he decided to disobey this order and march on Rome. The legal boundary to his province of Gaul was a stream called the Rubicon. By crossing the Rubicon Caesar made the first move in his march on Rome. In this sense we speak of a man "crossing the Rubicon" when we wish to say a man has committed himself to a new course of action. The Senators were alarmed and turned to Pompey for help, but as soon as Caesar arrived in Rome he was made consul. He still had to deal with Pompey, and Caesar defeated him at the battle of Pharsalus in 48 B.C. Between 48 and 45 B.C. Caesar conquered the remaining parts of the Mediterranean world.

Apart from his conquests he planned the rebuilding of Rome, the improvement of roads, introduced the Egyptian Calendar and reformed the government of cities. In March 44 B.C. he was murdered. Julius Caesar was a very talented man, a statesman, a general, an orator, a historian, a mathematician and an architect, but to gain power he chose to start a civil war. This should be borne in mind when judging how great a man was Caesar.

In the disorder that followed the death of Caesar the leading conspirators, Brutus and Cassius, were killed in the battle of Philippi. Rome began a period of orderly progress when Augustus became Emperor in 31 B.C., but the Emperors who followed Augustus included some of the most notorious rulers. They included men such as Caligula and Nero.

Caligula

Caligula, who was murdered at the age of twenty-nine after ruling for three years, was a monster. Like any bully with complete power over people, he got his entertainment from the misery he inflicted on others. Because of the baldness of his head and the hairiness of his body, the death penalty could be given to anyone who looked down on him or mentioned goats in his presence. He fed his wild animals with criminals to save the expense of butcher's meat, he forced his father-in-law to cut his own throat, he had innumerable people killed for the flimsiest of reasons. Only Nero could match him for crimes.

Caligula

Nero

Nero was one of the worst rulers in all history and Rome suffered his rule from A.D. 54 to 68. A waster on a grand scale, a coward and a murderer, he ruled in what has been called the first of the two centuries of peace! The following description from "The Twelve Caesars" by Suetonius gives some idea of his wastefulness.

Nero

"He built a palace, stretching from the Palatine to the Esquitine, which he called 'the Passageway', and when it burned down soon afterwards, rebuilt it under the new name of 'The Golden House'. The following details will give some notion of its size and magnificence. A huge statue of himself, 120 feet high, stood in the entrance hall, and the pillared arcade ran for a whole mile. An enormous pool, more like a sea than a pool, was surrounded by buildings made to resemble cities, and by a landscape garden consisting of ploughed fields, vineyards, pastures and woodlands—where every variety of domestic and wild animal roamed about. Parts of the house were overlaid with gold and studded with precious stones and nacre (mother of pearl). All the dining rooms had ceilings of fretted ivory, the panels of which could slide back and let a rain of flowers, or of perfume from hidden sprinklers, shower upon his guests. The main dining room was circular, and its roof revolved slowly, day and night, in time with the sky. Sea water, or sulphur water, was always on tap in the baths. When the palace had been decorated throughout in this lavish style, Nero dedicated it, and condescended to remark: 'Good, now I can at last begin to live like a human being.'"

Many innocent people such as Seneca, his old teacher, were killed. He was responsible for the murder of his wife and his mother and after the great fire of Rome in A.D. 64 he welcomed the rumour that it was started by Christians and he had many of them tortured and killed. In some ways Nero was a reflection of all that was bad in the Roman character for both he and the Romans were delighted to watch the combats in the arena.

The heavy taxation necessary for Nero's lavish schemes and his infamous conduct led to a revolt. Nero fled and committed suicide. If it seems scarcely possible to believe in the deeds of such men then one has only to turn to the present century and read of the lives of Mussolini and Hitler. Mussolini, like Caligula, did not like people looking down on him, for he was bald and had a wart on his head, so he tried to popularise the close cropped head as a sign of vitality. Petty things which are laughable to many, can become the cause of death and political trouble when they affect the lives of tyrants.

If we only concentrated on life in the city of Rome and the mad cruelty of its rulers, we would not get a fair picture of the Roman Empire. The governing class ran the empire efficiently under good or bad Caesars. Typical of this governing class was Agricola, who served under Nero and succeeding emperors.

Agricola and Roman Britain

Agricola spent his youth in Provence where many of the veterans of Julius Caesar's eighth legion had been given holdings of land as a reward for their services. An indication of the popularity of Julius Caesar was the large number of tombstones in this area which carried his name. Seneca said of Agricola's father, who was killed by order of Caligula, that he was too good a man to be left alive.

Agricola was brought up by his mother and was educated at a school in Marseilles. When Agricola was only three, the Emperor Claudius sent his expedition to Britain and eventually, after nine years of war, the foremost British leader, Caractacus, was taken prisoner and led in procession through Gaul on his way to Rome. Possibly the eleven-year-old Agricola saw Caractacus when the procession went through Marseilles. Then, instead of playing cowboys and Indians, the young Romans would play the parts of soldiers of the legion who fought the savage Britons.

At the age of nineteen or twenty Agricola went to Rome and saw Seneca, chief minister to Nero, who had known and respected Agricola's father. Agricola wanted his help in obtaining a commission in the army and a posting to Britain.

A Celtic cross

38

As a result of this interview letters commending Agricola were sent to Paulinus, the Commander-in-Chief in Britain. Soon Agricola was sent to Britain where he complained that the weather was bad with frequent rain and fog. Unlike some young officers, who left the hard work to the veteran centurions, young Agricola learned all he could about the organisation of the Roman army and the sort of opponents who faced them in Britain.

Agricola was one of a Roman army which invaded Wales and finally reached the coast opposite to the Isle of Anglesey. Only the Menai Straits lay between the Romans and the remaining Britons. The Britons were urged on by the Druids, priests who cursed the Romans so that they would be rooted to the spot and so allow the Britons to cut them down at their leisure. No such thing happened, for at low tide the Romans marched across the shallow Straits and defeated the Britons.

The Druids fought like madmen, and some were thrown on to their own altar fires. The groves of the Druids, where they carried out their bloodthirsty rites, were utterly destroyed. No longer would men be stabbed in the back so that omens could be drawn from the twitches of death. The Roman conquest wiped out the evil and cruel religion presided over by the Druids. Some years later most of Wales was brought under Roman rule. The final conquest was left to Agricola when he returned to Britain in A.D. 78.

Agricola served in Asia and in A.D. 74 he became Governor of Aquitaine. Later, in A.D. 78, he was made Governor of Britain. During the time between the previous Governor's departure and Agricola's arrival in Britain a revolt had broken out. Soon after his arrival Agricola was in Wales leading his troops to a decisive victory which completed the conquest of Wales.

Agricola tried to improve affairs in Britain. He stopped the wrongful use of taxes, like the tax in corn levied by the Romans. The Britons had been forced in the past to give corn for army use whenever it was demanded. Some Roman centurions, intent on profit, and knowing that the army granaries were full whilst those of the Britons were empty, chose this time to demand corn. The Britons had to find corn of their own, or buy some. The only source of supply was the Roman army granary, so the Roman army provided the corn which the Britons had to give back. Thus the centurion had both the money and the corn.

This sort of behaviour was possibly one of the causes of the occasional revolt in Roman Britain. Agricola stopped many of

Celtic Brooches

39

these practices. He was fair to the Britons whom he conquered in the North. With Wales under control his next major campaign was in the north. As he marched northwards he established forts and aimed to conquer the whole of Scotland. Near to Perth in A.D. 84 he fought the famous battle of Mons Graupius and as a result he believed he had the rest of Scotland at his mercy. However he was not able to complete the conquest of Scotland or to invade Ireland as he had intended for he was recalled to Rome.

Agricola did not return to Britain and he died in A.D. 93. His achievement was considerable, for his conquests in Britain enabled the south especially to be developed. Towns such as Verulamium and Wroxeter were built; their design was ambitious and their size large. Roads and forts were constructed to improve and safeguard communications and commerce. Britain owed much to Agricola for these peaceful benefits of Roman occupation. Men such as Agricola were the real fibre of the Roman Empire.

Building

Life in the Provinces of the Empire

Before we deal with the fall of the Roman Empire we shall consider what went on in the provinces of Britain and Judaea.

Britain gained a great deal from Roman occupation but there were some losses, the most serious being the vivid Celtic art which practically disappeared in Southern Britain. Roman roads become a less obvious benefit when you consider the amount of slave labour which went into their construction. We readily condemn a twentieth century dictator for the misery he inflicts on people in an attempt to develop his country. We should bear this in mind if we are tempted to give nothing but praise to those who administered the Roman Empire.

Transport by Land

In Roman Britain the upkeep of roads fell on the community and the great Roman south-west road which ran through Wiltshire and Dorset was impressive and its eight-metre long central causeway alone gave some idea of the work necessary for its construction.

A Roman Villa

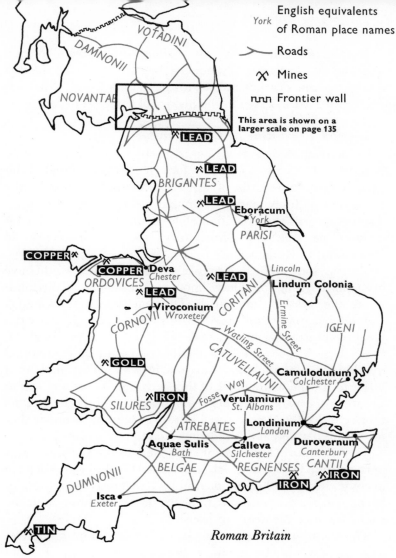

English equivalents
of Roman place names

York

‒‒‒ Roads

⚒ Mines

ᴖᴖᴖ Frontier wall

This area is shown on a
larger scale on page 135

VOTADINI

DAMNONII

NOVANTAE

BRIGANTES

⚒ LEAD

⚒ LEAD

⚒ LEAD

Eboracum
York

PARISI

COPPER ⚒

COPPER ⚒ Deva
Chester

ORDOVICES

⚒ LEAD

CORNOVII

⚒ LEAD

Viroconium
Wroxeter

CORITANI

Lincoln

Lindum Colonia

Ermine Street

IGENI

⚒ GOLD

CATUVELLAUNI

Watling Street

Camulodunum
Colchester

SILURES

⚒ IRON

Fosse Way

Verulamium
St. Albans

Londinium
London

ATREBATES

Aquae Sulis
Bath

Calleva
Silchester

Durovernum
Canterbury

DUMNONII

BELGAE

REGNENSES

CANTII

⚒ IRON

⚒ IRON

Isca
Exeter

⚒ TIN

Roman Britain

Metals such as tin, lead, iron, copper and even gold were
mined in Roman Britain, lead being of considerable importance
because silver was extracted from it and used to make coins.
Cloth, pottery and jet ornaments from the Whitby area were
other products of Roman Britain.

The major occupation, however, was farming and in the
countryside the most common building was the villa. Those
villas belonging to rich Romans would be luxurious but most
of the villas were at best comfortable, and at the worst no more
than cottages. It has been estimated that a villa excavated at
Ditchley was the centre of a farm of about four hundred hectares.
A plan of this large villa can be seen in the section on Building,
page 101.

Trade

Building

41

During the fifth century A.D. Rome lost control of Britain and the Anglo-Saxon settlements began. Many of the big estates became derelict and the towns were deserted. What has been called a Dark Age in the history of England began.

Judaea – The Rise of Christianity

Ideas

In the reign of Augustus Caesar, Jesus of Nazareth was born in Judaea. The written evidence for his life is to be found in the early Christian records of the New Testament and in the references to Jesus made by Roman writers such as Tacitus. Tacitus records the execution of Jesus but notes that after his death "the disease", Christianity, spread not merely in Judaea but to Rome itself.

Tacitus, son-in-law to Agricola, was a pagan and would have been amazed if he could have known of the history of Christianity in the following centuries. The teaching of Jesus had a tremendous impact on the ideas of his time though many did not take him seriously and took refuge in mockery. As H. G. Wells says, "he was like some terrible moral huntsman digging mankind out of the snug burrows in which they had lived hitherto. In the white blaze of this kingdom of his there was to be no property, no privilege, no pride and precedence; no motive indeed and no reward but love. Is it any wonder that men were dazzled and blinded and cried out against him?"

The Roman Government's answer to Christianity was persecution. The cross which the Romans thought should have become the symbol of the death of a dangerous revolutionary became instead a symbol of hope for mankind throughout the centuries since the death of Jesus.

The historian can record the spread of Christianity, but can only suggest why Christianity spread rapidly in the Roman Empire. Firstly, the age of Constantine was a very religious one when people were intensely interested in a life after death. Secondly, old ideas were breaking down and life in the Empire was hard and dangerous. Taxes went up, money lost its value and agriculture, the key industry, declined. Against this background Christianity gave many people some hope.

A large number of religions flourished before Christianity became the established religion of the Roman Empire. They ranged from the crudest animal worship to the cult of Mithras which became common in Europe in the first century A.D. Mithras was the god of heavenly light, an upholder of justice and truth. The main incident in his life was the slaughter of a bull from whose body all plant and animal life was supposed to

Constantine

42

Mithras slaying a bull

have sprung. The rites of this religion were often carried out in caves or crypts where the worshipper, after eating a sacramental meal of bread and wine, crouched beneath a grating. Above the grating a bull was slaughtered and the fresh blood gushed on to the worshipper below, who gained the vital force of the bull. Those who understood and accepted the mysteries of this religion gained eternal light in heaven.

Christianity in some ways resembled the mystery religions and this may have helped it to spread. Religions were regulated in the Roman Empire, but control was generally slack. One difference between the Christians and the followers of other religions was that they refused to worship other gods. Followers of other religions would not only change gods, but sometimes worship their own personal selection of the gods available. The Christians were clannish, developing a strong community sense which soon made their pagan neighbours dislike them. Being devoted to Jesus, who had been executed as a revolutionary, made them even more dangerous in the eyes of pagan Romans. The Christians were told that if they persisted in their religion they would forfeit their lives.

In A.D. 303 the Emperor Diocletian began a thorough-going persecution of the Christians. He ordered the destruction of their churches and scriptures and the ending of Christian worship. Torture, imprisonment and death were common, but instead of disappearing, Christianity increased its hold on the people of the Roman Empire. In the reign of Constantine, A.D. 324–337, Christianity became the official religion of the

43

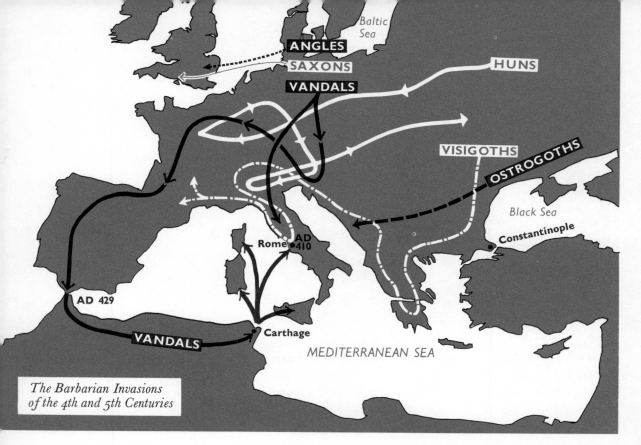

Roman Empire and this was a momentous change. Constantine's other very important decision was to found the city of Constantinople.

The Fall of the Roman Empire

The Roman Empire did not fall solely because it was attacked by barbarian tribes from East Europe. The stubborn resistance which Hannibal encountered when he marched through Italy appears to have gone by the fifth century A.D. The Roman Empire fell partly because it was internally weak and partly because it was attacked by barbarian tribes. For many years the Romans had allowed barbarian tribesmen to enter their empire. Most of these were German people who were adventurous fighters who preferred to add to their land holdings by conquest rather than by clearing the forest.

To the east of these peoples, as you can see on the map, lay the land occupied by the nomad horsemen of Central Asia and S.E. Europe. These people were more dangerous and destructive than the Germans. They had been turned westward by the Chinese who had built the Great Wall to defend their Empire. In the fourth century A.D. the Huns, the most dreaded of the

The Great Wall of China

nomad horsemen, had reached the Volga and the Oxus rivers and were driving other people such as the Goths on to the frontiers of the Roman Empire.

These horsemen were thick-set and tough, often bandy-legged and their eyes were slanted like the Chinese. They were fearless and cruel and spent most of their time on horseback. During the year they moved from the winter pastures in the south nearly two thousand kilometres to the summer pastures in the north. They were at home in this green ocean of land of Central Asia, where good horses and a portable house provided practically all their needs. Their favourite food was kumiz, fermented mare's milk, which was carried in leather bottles slung from the saddles of their horses. Their tents were made of a framework of rods covered in felt. In battle, one of their tactics was to flee from the battlefield and draw their opponents into a difficult position, only fighting at close quarters when the enemy was exhausted.

Typical of the Huns was their leader Attila, a short, tough, flat-nosed, sunken-eyed man who devastated much of Eastern Europe. His boast was that nothing grew where his horse had stood. He had no constructive ideas, his life was dominated by conquest, slave hunting and looting. He failed to take Gaul and died in A.D. 453. After his death the power of the Huns declined.

Attila the Hun

The First
Europe

The First Europe

During the period A.D. 400 to A.D. 800 what has been called
The First Europe came into existence. The centres of the first
Europe were in France, the Rhine country, England (a new
name) and Northern Italy. Unlike the Roman Empire it was
not a collection of countries which surrounded the great sea, the
Mediterranean. The lives of people in the First Europe were
very different from the lives of those who lived in the cities of
the Roman Empire. They were not town dwellers and scorned
the well-planned Roman towns, preferring to live in the
countryside. In the countryside these barbarians were equipped
with many things that were important to comfort and success
in the heavier lands of Northern Europe. During the four
hundred years after the fall of Rome they developed the use of
soap for cleansing; the use of butter instead of olive oil; the
construction of barrels; the growing of oats and rye; and most   *Agriculture*
important the use of the stirrup and the northern wheeled
plough. Read pages 56, 89, 90, 137 and 145 and decide
whether these years are so lacking in progress as their name,
The Dark Ages, leads you to believe.

The Catholic Church played a very important part in the
history of the First Europe for it preserved learning and
provided a refuge for many men and women. Eighty kilometres
from Rome in Subiaco, on the site of a deserted palace built by
Nero, lived a hermit called Benedict. It was a difficult task to
reach Benedict's cave for it was situated in a cliff face, and his
food had to be lowered to him on a cord. He lived there for three
years and then moved to Monte Cassino, a lonely and beautiful
mountain where he died in A.D. 543. St. Benedict wanted the
Goths and the Italians to be friends and he insisted upon hard
work and devotion. The Benedictine order of monks, the black   *Ideas*

47

monks, became the most important in Europe. Gregory the Great, one of the greatest Popes, was a Benedictine and during his term as Pope, A.D. 590–604 he raised the position of Pope to one of considerable importance in Europe. From his time onwards the Popes spoke with authority to the Kings of the Middle Ages, for Gregory behaved as a true successor to St. Peter.

The remainder of this story will largely be concerned with the history of Western Europe, particularly of Britain. Last time we talked of Britain was at the time of the Roman occupation. Before the Romans left, Britain was invaded by the Angles, Saxons and Jutes who landed in the south-east and east and by the Picts and Scots who attacked from the north.

The period between the fifth century and the Norman conquest in the eleventh century is one of the most troubled in British history. Life became very insecure and the ordinary man sought the protection of a stronger or wealthier neighbour, often becoming his "man". The lord would provide the protection whilst the man tilled the land. Often in Anglo-Saxon poetry the landless man was described as a homeless wanderer with little opportunity of personal happiness.

King Arthur

One figure, the legendary King Arthur, stands out in the years of the English conquest, largely because so much has been written in story form about him, but little is known in fact about this man. There is a Welsh story of the eleventh century which describes the deeds of this king and his knights. They perform many difficult tasks for a giant to help a young man win the hand of the giant's daughter in marriage. In one exploit Arthur saved some ants from a fire and in return the ants, within the space of a day, collect the correct number of flax seeds asked for by the giant. The story ends with a lame ant bringing in the last seed just at nightfall, a perfect ending.

The legend of Arthur was possibly built on the memory of a successful British or Roman leader who won battles against the invaders, in particular the victory for the British at Mount Badon somewhere in the South of England. The Britons certainly continued to live independently in the west in Cornwall and in Wales, but the rest of England fell to the invaders.

The Anglo-Saxon Invasions

Since little is known about the Angles, Saxons and Jutes, we have to use our imagination, and what little evidence we can get about their arrival in Britain. You can see on the map

A brooch of the 6th Century

48

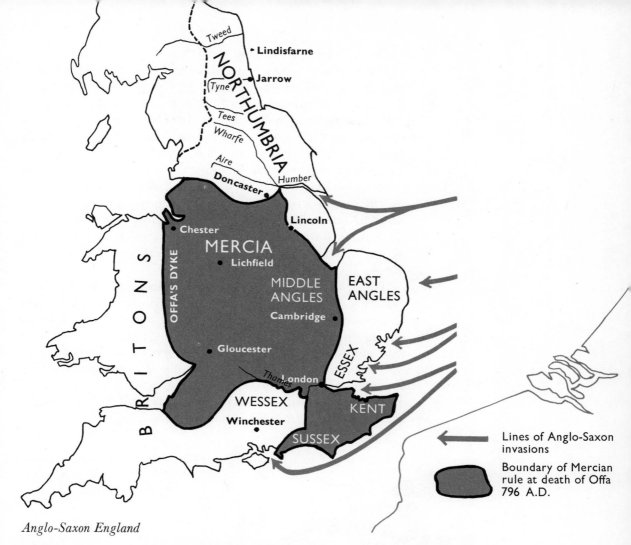

Anglo-Saxon England

their places of arrival; let us follow the imaginary route and experiences of one shipload of invaders.

They would come to the east coast of Britain and would sail up a river until they reached a likely place to settle, probably an open patch of gravel by the river. If they met no resistance they would use all their time to cut down sufficient trees to build their first rough huts, which would have a framework of wood covered with wattle and daub. They may very well have taken over deserted British fields at first, but as soon as they could make their own heavy ploughs and find beasts to pull them they could cultivate the heavy clay lands which lay in the midland area of Britain. Mercia was a strong central state set up by these invaders. It was made up of a large number of settlements drawn together under one lord, or king.

Agriculture

The Conversion of the English

The Saxons were heathen and the only Christians in England would have been the surviving Britons. One Christian, Patricius, was carried off to Ireland by a band of Scots in the fifth century and, known as St. Patrick, he converted many of the Irish to Christianity. His followers lived simply and later in A.D. 563 Columba, another Irish monk, crossed to England and established a centre for missionary work at Iona. These Irish missionaries gradually extended their influence in the North, but in A.D. 597 the Pope, Gregory the Great, realised what had been for him an ambition for over twenty years; this was to send a mission to England. Augustine was sent from Rome by Gregory to attempt the conversion of the people of Kent.

The king, Aethelberht, was suspicious and thought Christianity a sinister religion, so he insisted on meeting Augustine under the open sky. He became convinced of the sincerity of the missionaries and gave them a dwelling place at Canterbury. The most important convert Augustine made was Aethelberht. New churches were built and steadily and peacefully a new sort of invasion from Rome spread. Augustine was perhaps not the greatest of saints, but his steady work converted the South of England to Roman Christianity.

The ruins of Lindisfarne Priory, off the coast of Northumberland

In the North of England Paulinus won converts and later Aidan, a monk from Lindisfarne, completed the work. The two Christian churches, Irish and Roman, were different and could have become rivals, but after a meeting, or Synod, at Whitby in 663 the Roman Church triumphed. The Archbishop of Canterbury was the primate, or head of the church in England from this time.

The learning and gentleness of the monks of the Northern monasteries still played an important part in British history. Best known of these monks is probably the Venerable Bede, who wrote a history of England from the monastery at Jarrow on Tyne.

The Venerable Bede

A replica of a Viking ship made in Denmark

51

The Vikings

The gradual building up of the kingdoms shown on the map on page 49 took place before the coming of a new danger to the whole island. This danger was the Vikings. The monastery at Lindisfarne was attacked and sacked in 793 and more attacks on the north-east coast soon followed. The monasteries were surprised by these attacks, so were the Vikings but in a different way, for these rich monasteries were not defended and the monks were unarmed. York was famed for having one of the most magnificent libraries in Europe in the eighth century, but it was destroyed by the Vikings.

These fierce raiders came from Norway, Sweden and Denmark. Their raids extended westwards to the Faroe Islands, Iceland, Greenland and even the Atlantic coast of America, and southwards to the Black Sea, the Caspian Sea and the Mediterranean. Foremost amongst their gods was Odin, so keen on being wise that he sacrificed an eye and even hanged himself to gain knowledge. He was the god of battle, his spear was Gungner and he had a great, fleet, eight-footed horse, Sleipne. He was guarded by two wolves and was brought news from all quarters of the world by his two ravens. Only those who were dying on a battlefield saw him, a terrible one-eyed man in a cape and broad-brimmed hat. The customs and beliefs of the Vikings were like their gods—warlike and violent. Some of their dead were given a ship funeral by burning.

Charles The Great

Before the reign of Charles the Great, Charles Martel had prevented the Arabs from conquering much of Western Europe by defeating them at the battle of Tours in A.D. 732.

If you look at a map of the Muslim Empire you will see how the boundaries in the Mediterranean world changed between the fall of the Roman Empire and the time of Charles the Great. The Arabs had conquered a vast area which stretched from Spain in the West to the borders of China. They were enthusiastic to spread their Muslim religion throughout the world and soon the Arab lands became the centre of learning.

Learned men in Cordoba, Spain, could exchange ideas with their fellows in Cairo, Baghdad and Samarkand. The simpler Arabic numerals, the ones we use to-day, ousted Roman numerals. Algebra, an arabic word, and the zero sign came into use. The neglected works of Greeks such as Aristotle were studied and there is not much doubt that the Arabs had more discoveries to their credit at this time than their counterparts in

Bust of Charles the Great in gold and enamel Aix-le-Chapelle

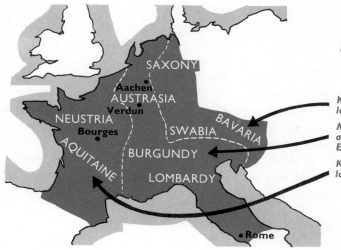

The Treaty of Verdun 843 A.D.

The break-up of the empire of Charles the Great

Kingdom of the East Franks later to become GERMANY

Middle Kingdom of the Franks an area disputed over by the East Franks and the West Franks

Kingdom of the West Franks later it became FRANCE

the West. Bear this in mind when you read about the Crusades, for to an Arab these attacks by Christian armies may well have seemed barbarian invasions.

The Muslim danger to Europe was not so great when Charles became king of the Franks in A.D. 768. The kingdom of the Franks with its Christian religion was the most important in Europe in Charles' time. To the north-east of this kingdom lay the Saxon lands. The Saxons had changed little since the time when many of their kind had joined in the Anglo-Saxon invasion of Britain. Charles wanted to conquer and convert the Saxons, but it took him years to do it, and then having conquered them by force he converted them by force too. Once Christians were persecuted, now a Christian Emperor persecuted others; the wheel had turned full circle. Charles was merciless on occasions, ordering the massacre at Verdun of 4500 Saxons who surrendered. He established Christianity by the sword not only in Saxony, but in the land of the Avars. His earlier conquest of the Lombards of Northern Italy had brought an understanding between Charles and the Pope.

Charles died in A.D. 814 at his palace at Aachen. Like Alfred, he had gathered a number of learned men about him, including Alcuin the Northumbrian. They had done a great deal to encourage religion, learning and efficiency in his dominions. There were blots on his character, such as his ruthless treatment of the Saxons, and his corrupt court. But his reign was one of progress and his character has become the source of some of the legends of the Dark Ages.

Government

53

The lands of Charles were divided into estates, each with its own lord. The estate books of the king describe down to the smallest detail what each person had to do for his land. The estate in some parts would be divided into farms, each farm containing ploughland, meadows, vineyards and orchards. The life of a peasant would be largely sleep and work, but hunting, holydays, festivals and the minstrels, beloved by Charles would give him some variety. Charles scorned grand clothing. He preferred something serviceable and plain—a jerkin of otter skin and a plain blue cloak. He travelled around his estates and wherever he went he and his court had to be provided for by his tenants.

King Alfred

The greatest king to rule in England during the period was Alfred of Wessex. By the time he ruled, from A.D. 871 onwards, the Danes or Vikings had ceased to carry out pirate raids. They had become settlers, and threatened to do to the Saxons what the Saxons had done to the British some centuries earlier.

Alfred was a lover of learning all his life and when a little boy, used to learn poetry by heart. When he was six he was sent to Rome and was blessed by the Pope. His careful upbringing helped to make Alfred one of the finest English kings, for he used his knowledge and power for the benefit of his people. The attacks by the Danes became more serious in his youth, for instead of raiding like pirates they stayed and aimed at getting as much land and possessions from the English as they could.

East Anglia was devastated by the Danes who then moved against Wessex in 870. At this time Alfred's brother Aethelred was king, and the two of them commanded the army which defeated the Danes at Ashdown. The Danes were forced back to their base at Reading. Aethelred died in April 871 and Alfred became king, although his brother had children who could have succeeded him. Alfred's forces fought many battles against the Danish host in this year, and at the end Alfred was forced to buy a temporary peace from the enemy.

The Danes were like a plague of locusts, living off the lands through which they passed. Wessex was left alone until 875 and 876 when the Danes made their second attack. Alfred had a scheme to counter the Danish attacks; he began to build a navy which could harass the Danes at sea. In 877 the Danes retired from Wessex, but in the next year a Danish army under Guthrum made a third and nearly successful attack upon Wessex. By Easter 878 Alfred was back in a fortification on the

A Saxon bowman

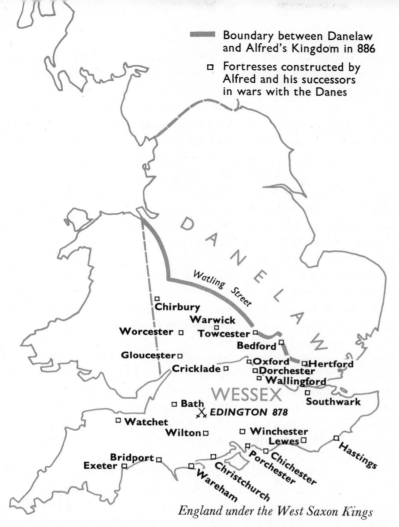

DANELAW

Watling Street

□ Chirbury
Warwick □
Worcester □ □ Towcester
Bedford □
Gloucester □ □ Oxford □ Hertford
Cricklade □ □ Dorchester
□ Wallingford
WESSEX
□ Bath Southwark □
X EDINGTON 878
□ Watchet
Wilton □ □ Winchester
Lewes □
Bridport □ □ Chichester Hastings
Exeter □ □ Porchester
Christchurch
Wareham

England under the West Saxon Kings

Isle of Athelney in the swamps which lay between the Mendip Hills and Exmoor in Somerset. It was here that Alfred burned the cakes, a trivial matter which is regularly recorded, whilst some of Alfred's great achievements are left out. From these swamps Alfred launched a counter-attack and eventually at Edington Alfred defeated Guthrum and the Danes.

Guthrum agreed to leave Wessex and during the talks between the two leaders the Dane was baptised and became a Christian. Guthrum and his followers went back to East Anglia and settled there while Alfred continued to strengthen his kingdom. He realised that his navy would have to be made even stronger and also that it was worth copying the Danish idea of fortified strongholds. To make sure each stronghold was properly manned, the men of the district had to help in the construction of the stronghold and man the defences when it was

A Danish raider

55

built. Alfred wanted if possible to allow the peaceful development of his land to continue side by side with the provision of good defences. He achieved this by a shift system. Each man living near a stronghold had to play his part in manning the defences in peace or war. A skeleton defence was maintained in peacetime so that the work of farming would not be interrupted, but when war threatened the defensive force was enlarged. These defences proved too strong for the Danes and their attacks were resisted. After Alfred's death the reconquest of Danish-held lands took place.

Alfred would be an excellent king if we judged him solely on his successful defence of Wessex, but he did more than defeat the Danes; he improved his kingdom. Learning was gradually disappearing from England when Alfred became king and he was determined to revive it by establishing schools and ordering the translation of books which could be used in the schools. Alfred translated many books himself, for he was a scholar as well as being a man of action. He improved the laws, one important change being his successful attempt to limit the blood feud. This custom, which obliged a murdered man's family to take revenge, was unjust and crude, but a reminder of the character of many of Alfred's people. If any English king deserved to be an example to later kings it is Alfred, for driven to war, he fought so that his land should be secure for peaceful development.

Use Alfred as a yardstick to judge some of the monarchs who have received far too much praise for their so-called adventures. Alfred's life is summed up in his own words, "My will was to live worthily so long as I lived, and after my life to leave to them that should come after me my memory in good works."

Alfred

The Middle Ages

The Norman Conquest

The Norman Conquest was the last successful invasion of England. Others have tried, Philip II of Spain in the sixteenth century, Napoleon in the nineteenth century, and Hitler in the twentieth century—but all of them failed. Why then was the Norman Duke successful?

To answer this question we must first understand the state of England in the eleventh century. Edward the Confessor, a saintly king, reigned between 1042 and January 1066. There is strong evidence for believing that he promised the throne to William of Normandy, for, apart from favouring Normans, he is alleged to have had a visit from William in 1052.

Among the powerful men of England in the Confessor's reign were Godwine and his sons. Godwine died in 1053 and his son Harald became Earl of Wessex. The death of the king posed the problem of who was to succeed to the throne. There were three possible candidates, Harald, Earl of Wessex, the man on the spot, Harald Hardrada, who claimed to be heir to Canute's kingdom, of which for some years England was a part; and lastly, William of Normandy. The struggles for thrones and the lands that went with them have been described as large scale robbery by some, and if any age justified this charge it is the one we are now about to study.

Harald, Earl of Wessex, was crowned King of England on the day Edward was buried and he governed England until his death on October 14th the same year, 1066. Harald Hardrada and Tostig, the younger brother of the king Harald, gathered a fleet of 300 ships and landed in Yorkshire. Harald, the king, marched swiftly north and on September 25th defeated the invading army at Stamford Bridge. Only twenty-four ships were needed to carry the survivors back. Harald Hardrada and Tostig were both killed.

Bayeux Tapestry—Preparations

Two days later the wind which had been unfavourable to the waiting force of William of Normandy changed, and William set sail for the south coast of England. News of the landing did not reach Harald until October 1st. He had a long march ahead of him, some 400 kilometres and as the army returned to the south he summoned extra men. William's force was small, but well-equipped and experienced, and many of his knights would be looking forward to handsome rewards in the form of land if the invasion were successful. William was careful to consult the Pope on the righteousness of his cause and portrayed Harald as a man who had stolen the English throne.

The Art of War

The forced march south from Stamford Bridge, a considerable feat, brought Harald and his men to Sussex by October 14th, the day of the Battle of Hastings, The English chose as their position a hill upon which the village of Battle now stands. This was a good defensive position. Provided the Normans had to carry the fight to Harald, the English could possibly have won the day at close quarters with their battle axes. William urgently needed a victory, for although he had had time to construct a coastal base at Pevensey, he could not afford to wait, for he might have the whole country in arms against him. The English shield wall held, but the early English successes led some of them to leave their good position to harass the retreating Normans. They were killed off by the Norman cavalry, which seems on at least one occasion to have drawn some of the English on to lower ground by pretending to retreat. The English centre held until Harald was shot in the eye by an arrow. After his death the English broke and fled.

Bayeux Tapestry— The Battle   58

William had to establish his rule in England and this was a difficult task. But he had his "secret weapon", a castle, not the solid stone castle of later years, but a quickly built fortification of wood. This could be erected on an existing hill or on a mound thrown up by Saxon levies. These early castles gave the Norman lords protection and enabled them to control large districts of conquered land. William deserved his title Conqueror for he won, and held on to his winnings.

Conisbrough Castle, Yorkshire

William I

William I

William could be as ruthless as Charles the Great when he felt it was necessary, and his devastation of the North of England was carried out with brutal thoroughness in 1069. The last of the Saxon leaders, Hereward the Wake, held out in the Fen Country, but was finally captured in 1071. By this date the Conquest was complete.

In 1086 William set about a careful study of his kingdom. The result of the survey was set down in the Domesday Book. The two volumes of this book are in the Public Record Office today. A bishop of Winchester described at a later date how and why this survey was done. He wrote:

"After consulting his council William sent men of proved discretion on circuit through the kingdom. A careful description was made of the whole country by these men, of its woods, pastures and meadows. . . . This was gathered into a book so that every man, sure of his own right, should not usurp that of another. The description was done by counties, by hundreds (a hundred was a subdivision of a county) and by hides (a hide was a measure of land of about 48 hectares) — beginning with the name of the king at the head and then one by one the names of the other great men. . . ."

From the Domesday Book we can see how clever William was for he did not give his barons whole counties as a reward for their support. He gave them scattered holdings of land which made it difficult for them to set up in joint opposition to the king. Furthermore, they would be kept busy moving from estate to estate.

The only barons allowed large united estates were the Earls of Chester, Shrewsbury and Hereford, all on the Welsh border. Their task was to defend the border, or to launch attacks on Wales. The barons were given estates provided they promised to be loyal to the king and to supply him with a force of knights when required. Even the church, one of the greatest land-owners, had to provide knights. The largest land-holders were the tenants-in-chief; below them came lesser lords, but each owed loyalty and armed support to the one above. At the bottom came the peasants, the free men, the villeins, the cottars and serfs.

The commonest were the villeins who had to work on the lord's land, called the demesne, from two to four days a week. They had to do extra work at harvest and other busy times. The freeman did not have to perform these services, but had to help the lord in the Manor Court. Freemen and villeins had

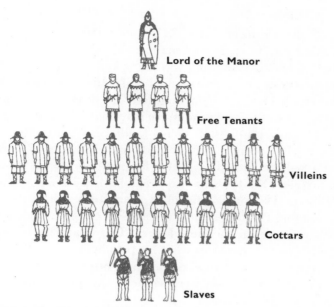

Lord of the Manor

Free Tenants

Villeins

Cottars

Slaves

The structure of society in medieval times

their own land, so did cottars, but they had much less than the other two classes of peasants. Serfs were not slaves, but they were the lowest type of peasant. The diagram shows you the order and dress of the different types of people in Norman England.

William I established order in England and ran the country efficiently. The Royal Treasury got its name, the Exchequer, from a black and white check cloth upon which money was counted. However, do not think this efficiency was for the sake of the people; its purpose was to enable the king to get the most out of his subjects.

Government

The New Forest was created in William's reign. The Forest Laws set down how the beasts of the forest were to be protected; wolves were to be killed off; inquests were to be held on the carcases of any beasts found in the forest; and anyone suspected of poaching was liable to be mutilated or killed. Hunting was the sport of the barons and woe betide any villager or forester who took the king's venison. The forest laws show the selfish and oppressive nature of Norman rule, while Robin Hood represents the cheerful side of forest life.

The establishment of a Norman king had one other important effect on English history; it involved England in the affairs of Europe for the next four centuries for, do not forget, William was Duke of Normandy as well as King of England.

William's Successors

William I decided that Robert, his eldest son, could not govern England, so he was made Duke of Normandy. William Rufus, his favourite son, was made king. He left his other son, Henry, over two tonnes of silver, a sizeable sum. Whilst William lay dying Henry, true to character for he was a grasping man, weighed out the silver to make sure that it was all there.

William I's division of his lands caused trouble. Norman barons had Robert as their lord for their estates in Normandy, and William II as their lord in England. As soon as the brothers quarrelled the lords had to break faith with one or the other. William II gained control of Normandy while Robert was crusading. William died before Robert returned, killed by Walter Tirel in the New Forest. The treatment of the king's body possibly shows us what his people thought of him. It was left in the forest until some peasants put it in a rough cart and brought it to Winchester, where it was buried without ceremony beneath a tower.

Henry I ruled from 1100–1135. He promised to behave better than Rufus had done. Robert attempted to take the English throne, but Henry bought him off and later when he was strong enough invaded Normandy. Robert was imprisoned and eventually died in Cardiff Castle at the age of 80.

Henry I lost his only son in a shipwreck. His daughter Matilda was left to succeed him in 1135. Many barons decided that Stephen, son of Henry I's sister, would make a satisfactory king, and put him on the throne instead of Matilda. Matilda married the Count of Anjou and so wed into "the Devil's Brood." The story of how this family were supposed to be related to Satan is as follows. One Count of Anjou returned from a journey with a beautiful lady whom he later married. They were happy and had four children, two boys and two girls. Only one thing appeared strange to the Count, his wife's refusal to attend Mass. The Count told four knights that next time the Countess entered the chapel they were to keep her there, even if they had to keep their feet on the hem of her very long cloak. The Countess cried out when they held the cloak, struggled free, and was never seen again. This tale was told in the twelfth century and many believed it was proof that the Counts of Anjou were descended from the Devil.

Henry II

After the civil war of Stephen's reign the first of the Angevin kings, Henry II, son of Geoffrey of Anjou and Matilda, came to the English throne. He had the uncontrollable temper which

Henry II

was the mark of "the Devil's Brood". Before he became king, he was married to Eleanor of Aquitaine. This was not a marriage for love, but for land, as Henry gained the province of Aquitaine. Eleanor was a prize worth having although she was eleven years older than Henry. The opportunity was too good to miss.

Stephen's death in 1154 might well have brought further struggles, but Archbishop Theobald took control of the country until Henry arrived in December. The barons soon noticed the restless energy of this young king; the only time he sat down was for meals and when on horseback. During the next year he rode throughout England, destroying unlicensed castles, settling disputes and setting his land at peace.

Henry II of Anjou—
Dominions and Dependencies

Becket

A king in the Middle Ages could keep his country at peace by a mixture of force and good organisation. Henry took the first steps towards modern methods of dealing with crimes and disputes. He sent his own judges to deal with all serious crimes in each shire just as modern judges do when they go "on assize". The judges tried to make sure that penalties for the same crime were roughly the same in each part of the country. Juries were started at this time as well. Henry's keenness to make sure that no crime escaped his courts led to his conflict with Thomas Becket, for the church at this time had the power to try its own officers. Henry gathered a lot of evidence that the church courts were far too lenient to offenders.

Becket was born in London, son of a Norman merchant, and was later employed in the household of Archbishop Theobald of Canterbury. He was an able and ambitious man and became Chancellor to Henry. The two men were great friends, and on the death of the Archbishop of Canterbury, Henry decided that he could extend his law to the church by promoting his friend to the vacant position. This seemed an admirable scheme, but Becket changed when he became Archbishop and championed the church against the king. Henry determined to get rid of Becket as Archbishop, and asked him to account for sums of money which had passed through his hands when he was Chancellor. Becket refused to hear sentence pronounced when he attended the king's council and fled to the continent.

Henry decided, as was the custom in Europe, to make sure there was no dispute over the throne when he died, by having the next king crowned whilst he was still alive. In the absence of the Archbishop of Canterbury, his son Henry was crowned at Westminster in 1170. This was an insult to Becket who, with the Pope's support, suspended all the bishops who had helped Henry. Becket returned to England in December 1170 while Henry II was still in Normandy.

When Henry heard of these things he was so angry that he as good as ordered Becket's murder. Four knights did the king's bidding and arrived at Canterbury before the king could recall them. The knights found Becket in the Cathedral and attempted to drag him outside so as not to commit murder on consecrated ground. A monk tried to defend Becket but Hugh of Horsea, nicknamed the Evil Deacon, drove his sword through Becket's head. After the murder the knights sacked the Archbishop's Palace. When the body was prepared for burial the hair shirt of the penitent was removed. Underneath, his back was covered in scars. During the Middle Ages devout men

64

underwent personal hardship and pain to prove that the spirit was stronger than the flesh.

Henry's last years were troubled ones. His sons were eager to get rid of him and they rose in rebellion. When Henry died in 1189 he was succeeded by Richard, and not by the young Henry. Young Henry had died in 1183. Richard spent much of his time fighting in the Crusades and the French king took advantage of this fact.

The Crusades

When Charles the Great ruled in France the Arabs still had a vast kingdom and at first Europe was not strong enough to think of launching a full-scale attack on them, but by the twelfth century the Arabs had been overthrown by the Turks. The Turks ill-treated Christian pilgrims, whereas the Arabs had allowed them to travel safely to Jerusalem. The Crusades were in some respects the attacks of courageous and greedy Christians upon an older and more advanced people.

The fourth Crusade, for instance, was one of the worst examples of greed. It began with an attack by the Crusaders on the city of Zara, rival to their city of supply, Venice. The sly Venetians not only profited from the sale of supplies, but got the Crusaders to do their dirty work of attacking a rival city. *Trade* As if this was not enough, the Crusaders followed it up by taking Constantinople, the capital of Byzantium, the country they were supposed to help. Eventually in 1458 the Turks took Constantinople. The Byzantine Empire fell and the Christian peoples of Europe no longer tried to gain the Holy Land. The two maps on page 68 enable you to judge what happened between the end of the First Crusade and the capture of Constantinople.

A Crusading Knight's Story

"I had heard one of the songs of the Second Crusade while visiting my estate in Normandy, and I could not get the words out of my head, 'God had ordained a tournament between Heaven and Hell, and sends to all his friends who wish to defend him, that they fail him not'. I decided that I must go on a crusade. What a joy it would be to help to retake Jerusalem.

King Richard came to Normandy in December 1189 and I joined him. By March 1190 he had collected a fleet and issued stern orders for the upkeep of discipline. Those who killed anyone on board ship were to be tied to the dead man

Richard I

E

A ship of the 12th century

Crusading armour

Siege tower

and flung overboard, and thieves were to have their heads shaved and covered with boiling pitch and feathers and cast ashore. These orders made men reserve their energies for the Saracens.

We travelled by land while the fleet sailed for Marseilles. When the king reached Tours he was given a pilgrim's staff. On reaching Marseilles we found the main fleet had not arrived so Richard got more ships and sailed for Sicily, leaving instructions for the main fleet to follow. The steering oars seemed clumsy instruments for guiding ships, but we managed and eventually reached Sicily.

This island gave some of us our first taste of Arab life, for the Arabs had held Sicily and had developed the island, planting lemon and orange trees and growing cotton and sugar cane as well. Ship building had led to the disappearance of much of the forest and the wild goats made sure that no trees grew to take the place of those that had been felled. The Sicilians were hostile and Richard took the town of Messina by force. Not until April 1191 did we leave Sicily, having been there since September 1190.

We reached Cyprus in May and again Richard took up arms, this time against the tyrant who ruled the island. Richard married Berengaria on this island.

Finally, in June 1191, we reached the coast of the Holy Land and joined the other crusading armies which were besieging Acre. We wore white surplices over our chain mail in an attempt to fend off the heat. Our horses were weak, the camp was filthy and I soon found the stories of scorpions and snakes were quite true, for these poisonous animals lurked to catch the unwary wherever we went. They are the Devil's creatures. As soon as our siege towers were in place we attacked and soon took Acre.

On August 2nd 1191 we began our march on Jerusalem and as we marched I was told of Richard's dealing with Saladin. He had even gone so far as to offer the Saracen leader his sister in marriage in an attempt to get a satisfactory agreement. The 2500 prisoners taken at Acre were drawn up in front of our armies, and beheaded in full view of the Saracens. This act will show them our intent to kill or to drive the unbelievers from the Holy Land. On our march we attacked an Arab caravan, gaining a great quantity of silk, spices and perfume, the last mentioned being of little use to the true crusading knight, who is unmarried.

Richard won the battle of Jaffa. In October Richard sailed

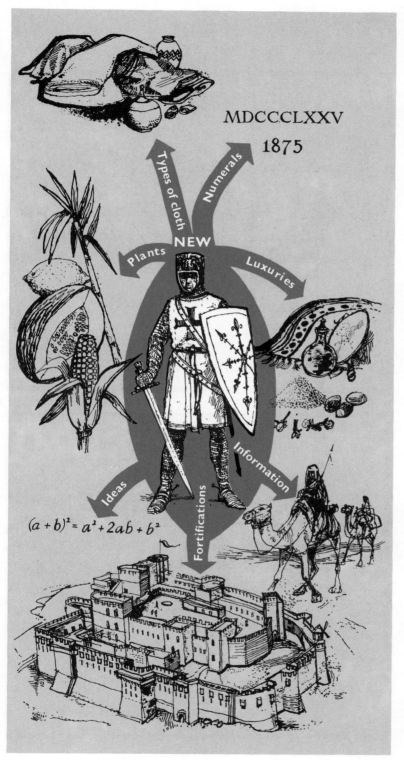

Types of cloth
Muslin and Damask, and
dyes such as lilac and
purple

Numerals
Arab numerals replaced
Roman numerals, e.g.
1875 instead of
MDCCCLXXV

Plants
Lemons, melons, sugar cane,
maize

Luxuries
Carpets and glass mirrors
Perfumes—musk and camphor
Spices—nutmeg, mace and cloves

Ideas and Information
Algebra, geography—increased
knowledge of the interior of
Africa

Fortifications
Concentric castles

*What Europe gained from
the Crusades*

for home, leaving some of us to make sure that the treaty he signed with Saladin, which safeguarded the pilgrims' route to Jerusalem, was carried out."

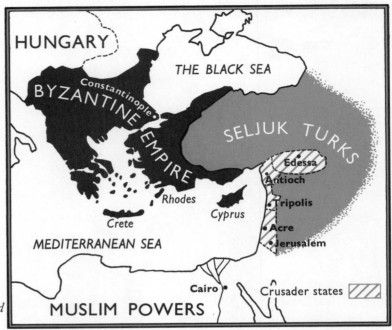

The Eastern Mediterranean World after the first Crusade 1099

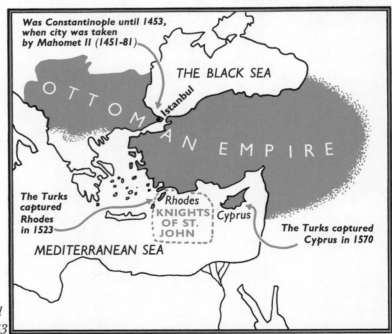

The Eastern Mediterranean World after the fall of Constantinople 1453

68

Crusader Castle—
Le Krak des Chevaliers, Syria

John

During John's reign, 1199–1216, the empire gathered by his father Henry II was nearly all lost. Philip Augustus, the French King, took most of John's continental possessions between 1203 and 1205. This was not the only trouble John had, for he quarrelled with Pope Innocent III over the choice of Archbishop of Canterbury. The Pope laid England under an interdict which meant that the services of the church, marriage, baptism and burial could not take place. Sermons were preached in the churchyards and people were buried in woods or ditches. John eventually agreed to the Pope's terms.

John's struggles with the barons were ended by his seal being placed on Magna Carta in 1215. Any activity, for instance a game of tennis, is impossible without rules. Without rules government is likely to result in rule by the strongest men. There were laws binding lord and peasant, king and tenant-in-chief, but the tradition of obeying the law was not as strong as it is to-day. The barons wanted to curb John for their own interests and Magna Carta did this. One of its clauses however, has become the charter of liberty for all Englishmen; it reads, "No freeman shall be arrested, or detained in prison, or deprived of his freehold, or outlawed, or banished, or in any way molested; and we will not set forth against him, nor send against him, unless by the lawful judgement of his peers and by the law of the land."

John was a very energetic man, chose his administrators wisely and has probably been wrongly called the worst king of England. He died in 1216 and was succeeded by Henry III who was only a boy of nine when he came to the throne.

John

Wales

So far Wales and Scotland have only been mentioned when the Roman occupation was described and when William I was creating the Earls of the borderlands with Wales.

By 1272 much of Wales had already fallen to the English. Only the mountainous corner of the north-west and the counties of Carmarthen and Cardigan remained independent. These lands were ruled by Llewellyn, Prince of Wales, and his people were very different from the English. They lived in lightly constructed huts in the upland pastures during the summer, but sought more solid homes in the valleys during the winter. They were a hardy people, owing their Prince six weeks' service free of charge each year, and like the Scottish highlanders they used it on occasions for pillage.

The failure of Llewellyn to do homage to Edward I led to war beginning in 1277. Edward was the first English king to carry out a thorough conquest of Wales. Edward's great Welsh castles were built after the war ended. Beaumaris and Caernarvon castles were built to prevent any supplies reaching the

Edward I

Building

Beaumaris Castle, Anglesey

mainland from fertile Anglesey. The people of London knew of the end of Welsh resistance when they saw the heads of the Welsh princes on the Tower of London. Edward's son was officially proclaimed Prince of Wales in 1301.

Master James was Edward's castle designer, and was very well paid for the thirteenth century. He received three shillings a day.

Caernarvon Castle, North Wales

Scotland

Edward subdued the Scots as well as the Welsh, and was known as "the Hammer of the Scots". Scotland was scarcely a country, for the clansman was loyal to his clan rather than to his country. Edward I hoped to unite England and Scotland by the proposed marriage between his son Edward and "the Maid of Norway", daughter of Alexander III of Scotland. The death of the "Maid" ruined the scheme and there were in 1290 thirteen rivals for the Scottish throne. Edward was asked to help to make the choice and John Balliol was made king. Balliol did not prove as friendly as Edward hoped, as he made an alliance with France and soon England and Scotland were at war. Balliol was deposed and brought to England, after an English victory at Dunbar.

Sir William Wallace now led the Scots, but was beaten at

71

Falkirk by Edward's army. The campaign ended with the siege of Stirling Castle. An oriole window was constructed in a house nearby, from which the Queen and her ladies could watch Edward's new siege engine, the Warwolf, being used against the castle walls. Wallace was tried in London and dragged by a horse from Westminster Hall to the Tower, then taken to Tyburn where he was hanged and quartered.

In spite of these defeats Scottish resistance continued and another rising led by Robert Bruce broke out in 1307. Edward I died at Burgh on Sands on the way to put down this rising.

Edward II disbanded the army and wasted the next seven years in idle court life. But in 1314 Edward II belatedly attempted to honour the promise he had made to his father to crush the Scots. A great army was gathered to invade Scotland, which by this date was ruled largely by Bruce. Edward's army was routed at Bannockburn by Scottish pikemen.

One of the important lessons the English learned from their

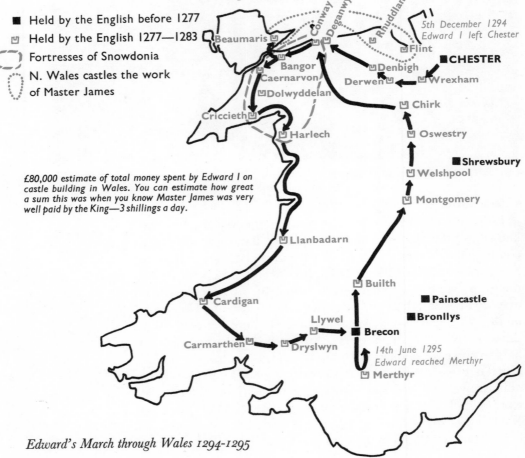

Held by the English before 1277
Held by the English 1277—1283
Fortresses of Snowdonia
N. Wales castles the work
of Master James

5th December 1294
Edward I left Chester

Beaumaris
Conway
Deganwy
Rhuddlan
Flint
CHESTER
Bangor
Denbigh
Caernarvon
Derwen
Wrexham
Dolwyddelan
Chirk
Criccieth
Oswestry
Harlech
Shrewsbury
Welshpool
Montgomery

£80,000 estimate of total money spent by Edward I on castle building in Wales. You can estimate how great a sum this was when you know Master James was very well paid by the King—3 shillings a day.

Llanbadarn

Builth
Cardigan
Painscastle
Llywel
Bronllys
Carmarthen
Dryslwyn
Brecon
14th June 1295
Edward reached Merthyr
Merthyr

Edward's March through Wales 1294-1295

campaigns in Wales and Scotland was the value of infantry. The Welsh longbowmen and the Scottish pikemen taught the English lessons which they used against the French at Crécy and at Agincourt.

England and France

The struggle between England and France for the control of the lands once held by Henry II lasted until 1558, when Calais, England's last possession on the continent, was lost. The fortunes of the two sides fluctuated. There were many years of peace, but always there was the risk that one country or the other would renew the war. Most of the fighting took place between 1328, the year when Philip VI of France came to the throne, and 1453, the date when Charles VII of France took Bordeaux and cleared all but Calais of the English.

There was no male heir to the throne when the French king died in 1328 and the French barons chose his cousin Philip to become king. The English court felt that the young Edward III should be King of France. But it was not until 1337 that the Hundred Years' War began. The English won control of the sea by the destruction of the French fleet at Sluys. In 1340, Edward followed this victory by the invasion of France. The small English army was victorious at Crécy, but this unexpected victory was dwarfed by an outbreak in England of Black Death, or Bubonic Plague, which no one could treat, and no one could check. From the military point of view Crécy was important, for a small English army, forced to fight a defensive battle, beat the French. Calais was taken on the return march, but the war was really a disappointment to the English. Edward did not become King of France although he put the fleur-de-lys on his coat of arms.

In 1356 Edward III's son, the Black Prince, raided Poitou, pillaging and burning. His force of 5000 or 6000, laden with booty, was driven to fight the French at Poitiers. As at Crécy, the English were outnumbered and had to fight a defensive battle. The Welsh archers, who were part of the English army, played havoc with the French cavalry and after three days the struggle was over. The victorious English marched back to Bordeaux with the French king as their prisoner.

When the Peace of Bretigny was concluded France had lost about one third of its territory. The next twenty years saw a decline in English strength and, with the death of the Black Prince in 1376, the French had an opportunity to win back much of their lost land.

Effigy of the Black Prince on his tombstone in Canterbury

73

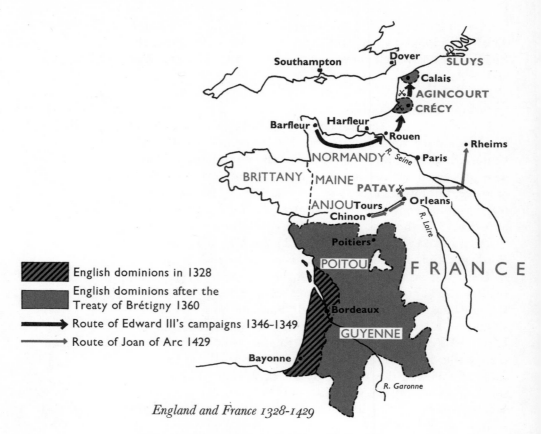

England and France 1328-1429

Legend:
- English dominions in 1328
- English dominions after the Treaty of Brétigny 1360
- Route of Edward III's campaigns 1346-1349
- Route of Joan of Arc 1429

Henry V and the Invasion of France

The next English king to make an attempt to gain the French crown was Henry V (1413–22). Henry and his army set sail for Harfleur in August 1414, hoping to capture the town and make it their base. Bad water, unripe fruit and too much local wine led to an outbreak of dysentery and over 2000 men died, nearly one third of Henry's army. Henry decided to march back to Calais. His biggest obstacle was the river Somme and Henry's tired men had to seek a passage over the river well away from its mouth. Once across, the French determined to bring the English to battle before they reached Calais.

The Art of War

Shakespeare's Henry V behaved very much as the king actually did before Agincourt, supervising every detail of the army's preparation for battle. The archers' positions were protected with sharpened wooden stakes driven firmly into the ground. The position chosen by Henry was such that the French had to attack on a narrow front. The early attempts of the French cavalry to ride down the English archers failed, for they were unable to get up any speed in the mud. The heavily

74

armoured French lay in heaps like stranded lobsters and Henry ordered his archers to take any handy weapon and kill them. The French army was cut to pieces and could no longer hinder the English march to the coast.

Henry's success increased his popularity and he was given a great welcome when he returned to England. He invaded France again in 1417 and his campaign was a series of sieges ending with the siege and fall of Rouen. In 1420 the Treaty of Troyes was signed. It provided for the marriage of Henry to Catherine of France. When Charles VI of France died, Henry and Catherine were to be monarchs of England and France.

In 1422 at the age of 35 Henry V died of dysentery and his nine months old son Henry VI was heir to two great kingdoms. The Duke of Bedford became Regent of France, a difficult, thankless, and expensive task.

Joan of Arc

It was now the turn of the French to triumph, and their recovery was due to Joan of Arc. Her faith, her peasant common sense, and the dangerous position of France led first the local squire and later the Dauphin to accept her as a saviour. The English had besieged Orleans for six months and their numbers had been reduced by desertion and sickness.

Joan and her captains raised the siege in the spring of 1429. Joan followed up this victory by insisting that the Dauphin should be crowned king of France at Rheims. Once crowned he set aside the claims of Henry VI of England. Joan was captured in 1430 by John of Luxembourg, a greedy Burgundian, who sold her to the Duke of Burgundy, who in turn let her be taken by the English. The trial of Joan of Arc, to us a tissue of lies and nonsense, was seen very differently by the Inquisition, who believed her to be inspired by the Devil. On May 30th, 1431, Joan of Arc was burned at the stake in the old market square at Rouen.

Between 1431 and 1453 the French recovered more of their land from the English, until in 1453 only Calais remained in English hands.

A bronze statue of Joan of Arc, Paris

The End of Byzantium

1453 also saw the end of the Byzantine Empire, much more important than the ejection of the English from France. The Turks under Sultan Mahomet II battered the walls of Constantinople with the heaviest cannon yet made, and in the next century threatened to take Vienna. By 1471 the Turks controlled lands which stretched from Asia to the Adriatic Sea.

The Wars of the Roses

The Wars of the Roses began in 1455 and were ended by the battle of Bosworth Field in 1485. In these troublesome years the lords of England seemed intent on committing suicide. Shakespeare's plays give a good impression of the effect the wars left on people's minds even a century after they had ended. His plays portray the horror of civil war with all its treachery and brutality.

Edward IV, a Yorkist, became king in 1461 after the overwhelming defeat of the Lancastrian forces at the battle of Towton. Order was restored, but events such as the restoration of Henry VI in 1470; the drowning of Edward's brother the Duke of Clarence in a butt of malmsey; and the murder of Edward's sons by Richard III showed that the horrors of the civil war lived on until Henry VII became king.

Edward IV employed his brother Richard as Lord of the North and the record of his work is different from the Richard Crookback of Shakespeare's play. Richard showed a great interest in justice and a kindness to nobles and to the common people. Richard reigned from 1483 to 1485 and died on Bosworth Field. "The Most Pleasant Song of Lady Bessey", a fanciful account of the events leading up to the battle described the death of Richard in these words:—

> "Besyde his head they hewe the crowne,
> And dange on hym as they were woode;
> The stroke his bacenett to his head,
> Until his braynes came out with blodde."

At Leicester the dead body was put on show for two days then buried in the church of Grey Friars.

Henry Tudor became king and like the true adventurer he carried no baggage, and so could use both hands to keep his crown on his head!

THE SECTIONS

Agriculture

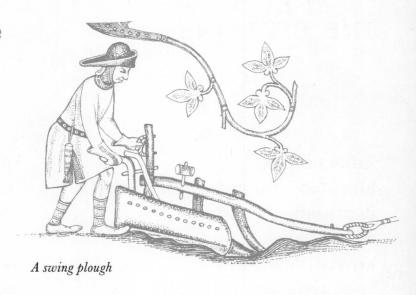

A swing plough

THE DEVELOPMENT OF SPECIAL TOOLS

As soon as mankind discovered the cultivation of plants and the keeping of animals they were able to lead a settled life, especially in the places where the early civilisations grew up. The food gatherers of the Old Stone Age brought nuts, grass-seeds and fruit into their camps and some seeds must have grown into plants around these sites after they had been dropped. It was a great step forward when some people planted seed year by year and harvested the crop when it was ripe. The cereals such as corn, rye and oats were grown and their cultivation led to the development of special tools.

The more harsh the climate, the more likely rye was to be grown for it was a hardy plant. In areas such as Turkey, where a mixture of rye and wheat is grown, rye spreads at the expense of wheat. Little wonder then that the Turkish peasant believes that wheat changes into rye. Vegetables such as cabbage, lettuce, spinach, nettle, cress, beans

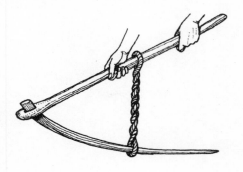

An Egyptian wooden hoe

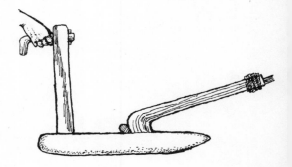

A scratch plough

and peas were also grown. Nettles provided food and were also used to provide a fibre which was made into nettle cloth. Apart from fibre, plants provided construction materials, vessels for drinking, and dyestuffs.

It was easy for men to plant and harvest their annual crops such as corn, but it was much more difficult for them to realise that new forests would have to be planted to avoid not only a wood shortage but the risk of the land being turned into a desert. Western Asia has suffered a great deal from soil erosion and even in the last century fertile parts of America were turned into near desert by bad farming.

It is easy to guess how the dog came to be man's companion, for dogs, like pigs, are scavengers. Man may have eaten his faithful friend in the past on a more widespead scale than he does today. [One of the places where dog meat is still a delicacy is the Burma frontier.] The dog was useful as a guard for man's flocks, herds or crops and in Tibet to-day guard dogs are an essential part of every nomad encampment. Other domesticated animals were the reindeer, goats, sheep, pigs, cattle, horses, asses and onagers. Man gained much from the domestication of animals for they were able to work for him, to give him food and clothing and to provide him with a means of travelling.

The picture shows you a Scottish crofter using a cas chrom which is a primitive farming tool. Even digging-sticks, the earliest type of tool for breaking up the ground, are still used in some parts of the world. Different materials were used to make tools, bone and ivory in Arctic regions, hard wood in the Pacific Islands, and iron in Africa. In most cases tools could also be used as weapons.

A Scottish crofter using a cas chrom

It soon became clear to the food gatherers that wild grasses grew near to streams and springs and as soon as man began to produce his own food he had to devise a means of watering the land. A special device for hoisting water was made in Ancient Egypt. This was the shaduf.

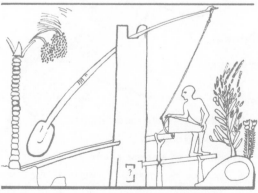

A Shaduf

F

Agriculture

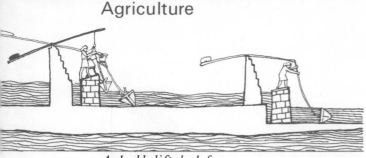

A double lift shaduf

These devices were used extensively in the Nile Valley and in the low-water season the shadufs had to be kept going for one hundred days so as to provide sufficient water for the crop.

Ensuring an adequate supply of water was a problem to army leaders, or to anyone arranging long journeys in the Middle East. Sometimes the problem was solved by digging wells, sometimes by storing water along the route as the Persians did when they invaded Egypt in 525 B.C.

Ancient Egypt. If we turn our attention to Ancient Egypt, one of the great civilisations of the Ancient World, we shall see how carefully life had to be organised. The following imaginary account of a day in the life of an Egyptian tax-inspector should give some idea of farming in the Nile Valley.

"I had been in this district twice before this year, once when the land was flooded by the waters of the Nile, and later when the fields were beginning to show the first blades of green corn. Now it is the third season of the year, the Harvest, and I have to measure the fields for the annual calculation of the amount each farmer will have to pay in tax. It is always a marvel to me why some farmers still use the old sickles with flint teeth set in a wooden haft, instead of investing in the sharper metal sickles. Some of the nobles who live by

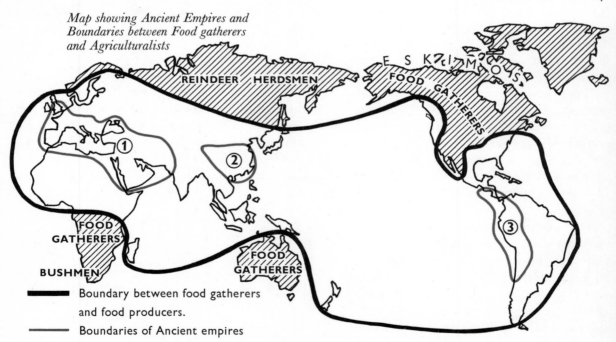

Map showing Ancient Empires and Boundaries between Food gatherers and Agriculturalists

▬▬▬ Boundary between food gatherers and food producers.

──── Boundaries of Ancient empires

1. Includes— *EGYPTIAN, SUMERIAN, PERSIAN, GREEK & ROMAN EMPIRES*

2. Includes— *CHINESE EMPIRE*

3. Includes— *MAYAN AND OTHER SOUTH & CENTRAL AMERICAN EMPIRES*

the riverside have splendid gardens with stone pools in the centre, containing live fish. The gardens provide these nobles with fruit, vegetables and flowers. Sometimes, when I have finished checking all the boundary stones round the estate, I am invited in to enjoy the shade of the summerhouse set among the pomegranate and fig trees. One thing I shall mention when I return to Thebes is the excellent state of the irrigation canals in this district."

OTHER CIVILISATIONS IN THE MIDDLE EAST

The Nile flood is more predictable than the floods of the Euphrates and the Tigris which can on occasion arrive early and bring a very large amount of water. The story of the Flood, told in Hebrew and Sumerian legend, has been shown by Sir Leonard Woolley, the archaeologist, to have been based on fact. He found an eight foot bank of clay in his excavations at Ur which was left there when the whole of the lower valley of the Tigris and the Euphrates was flooded. An area six hundred and fifty kilometres long and one hundred and fifty kilometres across must have seemed like the world to people of that time, so little wonder they talked of the world being flooded.

Keeping the canals in proper condition was a very important task, and the king Hammurabi wrote to one of his governors.

"Summon the people who hold fields on this side of the Damanu canal, that they may scour it. Within this present month let them finish it."

The fertility of the land of the two rivers amazed the Greeks, and it is not surprising, for two and sometimes three harvests could be gathered in one year.

One plant always associated with the desert area is the date palm, which had many different uses. The wood could be used in building, the ribs for furniture and the fruit as a main item of diet. The rich sugar content preserves the fruit, and it can be exported. The date stones provided charcoal, or could be pounded up and used as flour. The Bedouin of the desert said with justification, "Seven dates make a meal."

The engineers of Babylonia and Assyria had an extensive knowledge of flood control and in war they made terrible use of it. One of the methods of punishing a defeated enemy was to ruin his irrigation system. Sennacherib of Assyria vented his fury on Babylon in this way. He recorded that "Through the midst of that city I dug canals, I flooded the site with water, and the structure of its very foundation I destroyed . . . so that in days to come, the site of the city and its temples and gods might not be remembered. I completely blotted it out with water-floods and made it like a meadow."

Irrigation in an Assyrian park

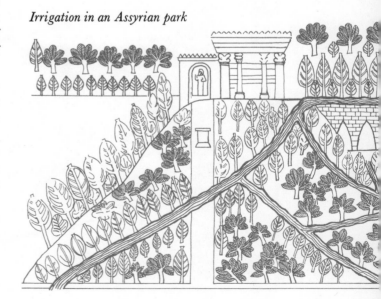

Agriculture

Ancient Greece

Ancient Greece with its broken coast-line provided numerous river valleys where wheat, barley, grapes and olives could be grown, while in the wet season the upland pastures would be used for grazing flocks of sheep. The earliest Greeks were shepherds, but between 1000 B.C. and 600 B.C. they became settled instead of nomadic and soon the city states were formed. It was in the matter of government and the arts that the Greeks excelled and commerce provided them with the materials and foodstuffs which they did not produce themselves.

The Roman Empire

If you look at a map of the Roman Empire in the second century A.D. you will see that the core is around the Mediterranean Sea. This area had only about 100 mm of rain in each of the summer months of June, July and August. Some parts such as Sicily were gradually turned into desert areas by lack of thought for the future. Trees were cut down to provide for the needs of ship builders and charcoal burners, and young saplings had little chance of replacing them because of the constant cropping by goats. The Romans faced the same problem as the Egyptians and Sumerians, that of conserving water. The method they adopted was to pulverise the soil with continual ploughing, so that it was broken up into very small particles. Present day experiments have shown that soil broken up in this way holds much more moisture than unstirred soil.

In Ancient Rome the sequence of work for the farmer was as follows: the land was ploughed in January or February,

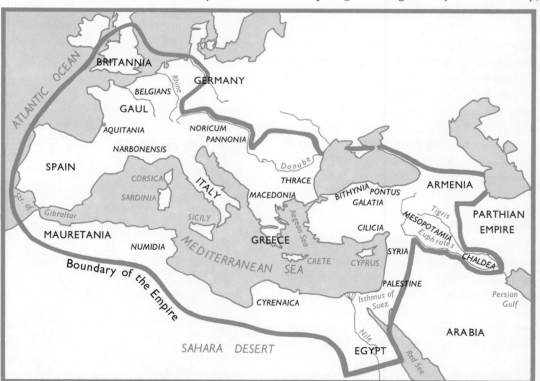

The Roman Empire in A.D. 167

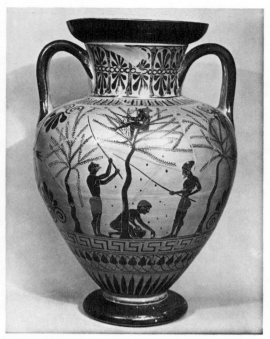

An amphora showing olive pickers

and often reploughed in March; during the summer it lay fallow, cleaned by a hoe or a harrow which was dragged across the fields; in October the land was ploughed again and sown. The seed germinated in the spring, and in Italy, June or July were the months when the harvest was gathered. Thus each field remained fallow every other year. Frequently only the ears of corn were cut off by the sickles, the straw being ploughed in to enrich the land.

Shade from the sun was important in growing many crops, and the incredible tale is told of a field at Tabace in Africa where olive trees grew beneath date palms, which had in turn beneath them, figs, vines and finally corn. The Romans took a lot of care of their crops, hoeing and weeding them regularly. The methods of threshing varied from the use of a stick to beat the ears, to the use of the farm oxen to tread out the grain.

The Romans grew fodder crops for cattle, such as lucerne, and a mixture of barley and other plants called farrago which the cattle ate green.

The Romans were well aware of the importance of fertilisers. Stable manure and the dung of birds, especially pigeons, was widely used. Shepherds often fired the pasture in summer for they knew the value of wood ashes in increasing fertility. The burying of lupins and bean stalks was advised by Cato, but these advanced methods of farming were not widespread and only survived in a few districts after the fall of the Roman Empire.

THE DEVELOPMENT OF FARMING AND FARM IMPLEMENTS IN THE MIDDLE AGES

The Field System

The attacks by raiders such as the Vikings in the Dark Ages led many people to seek the protection of a lord. The lord did his best to protect the families under his care. In return they served him in war by fighting in his army and in peace they tilled his land and provided for the lord's needs. This was a sensible bargain and a way of life which spread to many parts of Europe.

Many kings and lords had widespread estates and when they were not at war, they and their households spent much of their time travelling to their estates. They ate through the produce of each estate before moving on to the next. Even the famous emperor, Charles the Great, moved around his lands with a regular caravan of carts and horses.

When people had settled in one place, then they had to make sure that they did not exhaust the land. One way to do this was to give a field a rest for a year, to leave it fallow. Fields were generally left fallow once every three years.

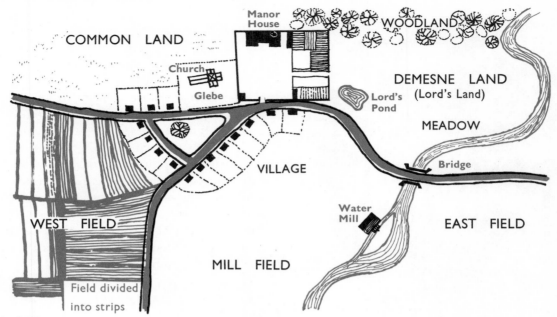

COMMON LAND

Manor House

Church

Glebe

WOODLAND

DEMESNE LAND
(Lord's Land)

Lord's Pond

MEADOW

VILLAGE

Bridge

WEST FIELD

Water Mill

EAST FIELD

MILL FIELD

Field divided into strips

A Manor

Aerial photograph of a field in Dorset showing medieval lynchets

The Medieval Manor

In the Middle Ages the English country-side was largely divided into manors. The land of the manor would be made up of arable land, which was farmed on the three field system: meadow, pasture land, woodland and wasteland. The main crops raised were wheat, rye, oats, barley, beans and peas, whilst the animals kept were oxen, sheep and pigs. The oxen were steady beasts of burden, and moreover they provided meat. The sheep were lean, scraggy animals and were raised chiefly for their wool, but also for their manure. The great difficulty in the way of successful stock raising was the lack of winter fodder. Some hay was gathered in the summer, but it was never enough to supply the needs of the beasts during the winter so that many of them had to be slaughtered in the autumn and their flesh was preserved by putting it in brine.

The short-woolled sheep were raised on the moors and hills, but the long-woolled sheep, which provided the finest wool, were raised on the richer grasslands. The accounts of the sheep farms of the Middle Ages were kept by the reeve or bailiff. In the spring, the lambing season, the shepherd would spend much of his time in the large stone sheephouse. Here he would look after the flock by day and night, making sure that plenty of milk was brought from the dairy to supply the weaker lambs. Later in the year washing and shearing took place, a job that some of the villeins might have to do. The shearing of the sheep was a great event and was followed by a feast. A thirteenth century writer said this of the shepherd's character and work:

"It profiteth the lord to have discreet shepherds watchful and kindly, so that the sheep be not tormented by their wrath but crop their pasture in peace and joyfulness; for it is a token of the shepherd's kindness if the sheep be not scattered abroad but browse around him in company. Let him provide himself with a good barkable dog and lie nightly with his sheep."

The People of the Manor

The Domesday Survey carried out by the officials of William I in 1086 showed that there were the following numbers of the main classes of people in English manors.

	Total
Lords of manors	9271
Free tenants	35 513
Villeins	108 456
Cottars	88 952
Slaves	26 362
Burgesses	7968

It is clear from this survey that the commonest class of people was the villein.

Many of the villages of the Middle Ages were deserted by the sixteenth century and

Ploughing

Breaking clods

Reaping

Threshing

Duties of a villein

until a short time ago many people did not believe some of them had even existed. One of the signs that these villages did exist is the presence of a fishpond, or a group of fishponds. It was difficult to get fresh fish to people who lived inland and so manors provided their own fish from fishponds. Often a stream was diverted to form a series of fishponds and then used to provide the driving force for a water mill. We might wonder how the peasant of the Middle Ages managed without potatoes, but he would be surprised to find how few of us had tasted freshwater fish such as eels, bream or carp.

87

Aerial photograph showing medieval fishponds, Harrington, Northants.

The main feature of the manor was that its inhabitants provided for almost all their own wants. They raised their own food and raw materials and made them up into finished goods such as clothes and shoes, so there was little need for them to trade with the outside world.

Drainage of land. The Dutch were the best drainage engineers of the Middle Ages, and of later times. Between 1200 and 1500 they reclaimed some 115 500 hectares of land. Before this land was drained it was in dispute between land and sea. The people had to build their homes on the high land and anxiously watched the water coming in as the tide rose to flood the lowland areas. Dikes were built and the drained areas were called polders.

FARM IMPLEMENTS

Scratch plough

Heavy plough

Ploughs. Sometimes films dealing with Southern Italy and other Mediterranean countries show a farmer ploughing his field with a primitive-looking plough drawn by oxen. The plough seems to be doing no more than disturbing the surface and breaking up the soil. Possibly you thought as you watched how an English plough could have improved on this performance. The improvement might not be so great as you thought, for this primitive plough was doing a special task, breaking up the soil into as fine a tilth as possible so as to cut down evaporation of water from beneath the surface. In Northern Europe, where rainfall is heavier and the ground can get waterlogged a very different problem faces the farmer, that of having too much water. The plough suitable for Northern Europe has to be strong enough to turn the heavy, wet soil over, and it should also help to drain the land. Scratch ploughs which just broke up the land were used in the Celtic fields in Britain before the Romans came. As cross ploughing helped to break up the land to a greater extent the fields were generally square in shape and were usually on the higher lands. On the other hand the fields of the Saxons were long and narrow and situated in the fertile lowlands where the heavy plough was used.

Parts of the plough

Coulter

Plough pole

Mouldboard

Plough-share

Sowing seed

Harrowing

Apart from the main framework and the handles the plough used in Northern Europe had three key parts. First the coulter, or heavy knife, which was set into the plough beam and cut vertically into the ground. Second, the plough-share which was set at right angles to the coulter and made a horizontal cut. Lastly, the mouldboard which turned the soil over. Mouldboards were not used until the eleventh century.

Seed sowing. The seed was broadcast, the sower walked to and fro across a field throwing seed out of a basket with a broad cast of his arm. Seed sowing machines were apparently used in Sumer many centuries earlier, but broadcasting was the method used in the Middle Ages.

Harrows. In Roman times harrows had two uses, to tear out the weeds and to cover the seeds. A triangular harrow was often used in the Middle Ages and in its absence a hawthorn tree was sometimes dragged across a newly sown field to cover the seed with soil. Another type of harrow was made of a log of oak fitted with iron spikes. It was used for breaking up rough ground.

Harvesting tools. Once iron came into general use, tools such as the curved sickle and the long handled scythe were made specially for harvesting. The long handled scythe was developed in Roman times. After the corn had been cut it would be stored and later threshed. The threshing was done with a hinged flail.

Baking pancakes in Egypt

Scythe

Hinged-flail

FOOD AND DRINK
Ancient times

The food gatherers of prehistoric times must often have been faced with starvation for they had scarcely any control over the animal and plant life of their world. The ability to preserve food helped them to avoid starvation. The fisher folk of the Arctic dried fish for the lean weeks of the year, whilst the hunters of America dried meat to make pemmican.

Later, as agriculture and stock breeding developed, mankind had the opportunity for even greater control over its own existence. The development of ovens, and of apparatus for grinding and crushing, the knowledge and use of fermentation and methods of preservation, led to great changes in human diet.

Ovens. The simplest oven in ancient Egypt was made from one or two stones laid flat upon a group of upright stones. A fire was lit between the upright stones, and was looked after by the cook. In Ur the temple kitchens had large clay beehive shaped bread ovens.

Tools for Crushing. The commonest ones used were the pestle, a club shaped tool, and the mortar, a vessel made of hard material which can stand up to the pounding of the pestle. Pestle and mortar

91

-= A Donkey Mill

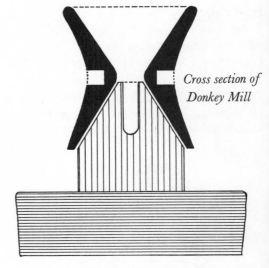

Cross section of Donkey Mill

were used for removing the husks of grain in Egypt. The housewife had the job of grinding the corn, and until the time of the Roman Empire saddle querns were used. A rubbing motion was used to grind the corn on these querns.

The diagrams show the large donkey mills found at Pompeii. The donkeys were harnessed to the hour-glass-shaped upper stone whose circular progress provided the power to grind the corn. The flour collected on the circular platforms below the grinding stones.

Presses. The press was invented to get the oil and juice from olives and grapes. The Egyptians used bag presses such as

the one illustrated. The bag containing the fruit to be pressed was suspended in the frame and the workmen then twisted the stick attached to the end of the bag. The juice was collected below.

The Greeks developed the beam press which used the principle of the lever. One end of the beam was fitted firmly between two stone pillars or in a hole in a wall. The fruit was put in bags or between pieces of wood under the middle of the beam. Then the other end of the beam was pulled down. Heavy weights were attached to the beam so as to increase the pressure. An improvement of the beam press was the screw press.

A bag press

A beam press

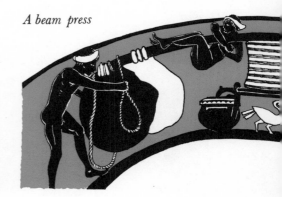

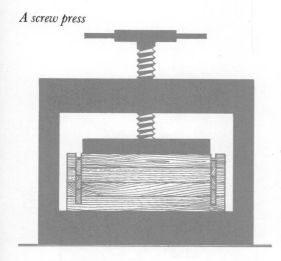

A screw press

Fermentation. This process takes place in the making of leavened bread and alcohol. When yeast is added to dough fermentation takes place. Honey produced mead when fermented, whilst date juice provided date wine. The workmen and officials in Sumer were given a ration of beer, and the more important the official the bigger was his ration of beer. The most important officials had as much as five litres a day!

Wine was produced in Egypt and other parts of the Middle East, but it was in Greece where the cultivation of the vine reached its highest level. Wherever the Greeks went they took the vine with them. On returning from his travels after seventeen years, Odysseus reminded his old father Laertes of an incident which took place when he was a little boy. His father had taken him through an orchard, telling him the names of the various trees, and had promised him thirteen pear trees, ten apple trees, forty fig trees and fifty rows of vines. This is some indication of the importance of the vine to the Greeks, in myth or in fact.

The other major crops were olives and wheat, the former providing olive oil, essential to the Greek housewife for her cooking.

Vinegar, the strongest acid known to the Ancient World, was made by allowing fermentation to carry on until vinegar was formed. Sometimes bread was dipped in dilute vinegar, but apart from this its main use in the kitchen was as a preservative.

Like the Greeks the Romans rated beer as a barbarian drink and Tacitus wrote of German beer as a liquid curiosity, "a liquor drawn from barley or from wheat and, like the juice of the grape, fermented as a spirit."

A Feast

These technical developments enabled men to enjoy a much wider variety of things to eat and to drink. Indeed the rich people in the Roman Empire must have been amongst the greatest gluttons in history.

Imagine three sloping couches around a large table with the fourth side left open for the servants to bring in the many courses which made up the meal. Guests were announced and ushered to their places and given knives, toothpicks and spoons of various shapes and sizes. Fingers were used instead of forks and after each course perfumed water in which each guest cleaned his or her hands was brought by slaves. Different wines were served between each course.

Now to some details of the dishes provided in the eight or ten hours of eating which made up the average Roman banquet. You may have amused yourself devising some fantastic menu which you never believed could exist, but the Romans turned their imagination into facts on the banqueting table. Writers describe dishes such as this one eaten at Trimalchio's feast. A tray, upon which there was a wooden hen in a basket was brought into the dining room by two slaves. The slaves hunted in the straw until they found some peahen's eggs which they gave to the guests. Each egg contained a small spiced bird cooked in the yolk of the egg. Such was the skill of the Roman chefs that one Roman, Petronius, said that his chef could make fish out of a sow's belly, chicken out of a knuckle of pork and a wood pigeon out of bacon.

THE MIDDLE AGES

The Muslim invasion of Europe during the seventh century and afterwards led to the introduction of such crops as rice and citrus fruit into Sicily and Spain, and later into Northern Italy and Southern France. By the tenth century many monasteries were growing hops which made a bitter beer very different in flavour from ale, which was sweeter. By the fifteenth century beer made from hops was by far the most common variety brewed in Europe.

Another change which took place in Europe was the increase in the production of cheese and butter. They became part of the daily food of the rich and were also enjoyed by some of the poor.

The diet of the mass of European people in the Middle Ages was simple and often sparse. A kind of soup was drunk in the morning and for the other meal of the day porridge or soup, fish and vegetables were eaten. Pastry was a luxury because fats were expensive. Fresh meat was not usually eaten more than once a week, but fish, dried or salted, was eaten much more than is the case nowadays. The drinks included water and milk and, if they could afford it, beer and wine.

Building and Town Planning

Egyptian workmen dressing stone

The people of the Old Stone Age who wandered in search of their food often lived in caves. Where there were no caves they built simple shelters to protect themselves from the worst of the weather. In Russia the mammoth hunters dug the ground to a depth of about sixty centimetres and in this hollow built an oval dwelling which may have had a tented covering.

The simple beehive-like structures built by the aborigines in the swamps of the Swan river in Queensland, Australia, give some idea of the sorts of temporary dwellings that primitive peoples lived in. These were constructed in the forks of dead trees in the swamps and a smoky fire inside kept away the mosquitoes; better to have streaming eyes than the constant attention of these dangerous insects.

The village settlements of Germany contained longhouses such as the one illustrated below.

Longhouses

Building

Woodhenge

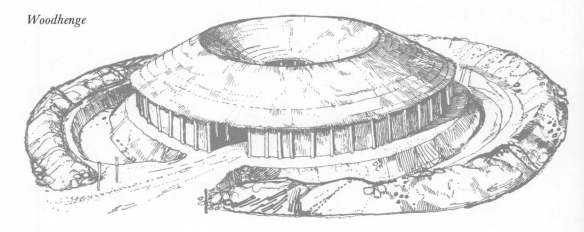

The remains of quite elaborate timber structures have been found in barrows (burial mounds) in some parts of England. An open air temple called Woodhenge is reconstructed in the illustration.

At Glastonbury in Somerset a lake village has been discovered and dug out. Many of the houses had as many as four floors; one had ten. These facts give some idea of the skill of the builders in Iron Age Britain.

EGYPT

In Egypt the earliest dwellings were made of reeds plastered with mud, but soon these were replaced by buildings with walls of rammed clay. The discovery that the baking of clay gave a longer lasting and stronger building material led to the widespread use of bricks. The Nile valley contains much fine stone. This became a government monopoly, so ensuring a plentiful supply for the construction of the

The Great Pyramid

fine buildings of Ancient Egypt.

The Pyramids, apart from being some of the greatest visible masterpieces of antiquity, give an insight into the craftsmanship of Egyptian builders. The Pyramids were sited to the west of the Nile on the side of the setting sun. They had to be fairly near to the river, for the stone used in their construction was brought from the quarries by ship. The site had to be solid and level. The Egyptians had an ingenious method of making sure that the rock base was perfectly flat. The site was surrounded by banks of mud from the river and the enclosed space was then flooded with water. Trenches were then cut in the submerged rock so that each trench was the same depth beneath the surface of the water. The water was released and the spaces between the pattern of trenches quarried down to the level of the trench bottoms.

The Pyramid had to be square at the base, and the difference in length between the longest and shortest sides of the Great Pyramid is only 19·75 cm; a very small error when you consider that each side is over 22 500 cm long. The blocks of stone used in making this Pyramid weighed about two and a half tonnes each and they were most likely taken from the quarries during the Nile's flood period so that they could be taken as close as possible to the building site by water. The stones were carried from the ships on sledges which were dragged over wooden rollers. Water was poured on to the rollers to lessen friction as teams of men dragged the sledges. A ramp would be built on the side of the Pyramid and the blocks would be dragged up until, finally, the capstone would be put in place. The stone was dressed by the masons as the ramp was taken away. This must have been in itself

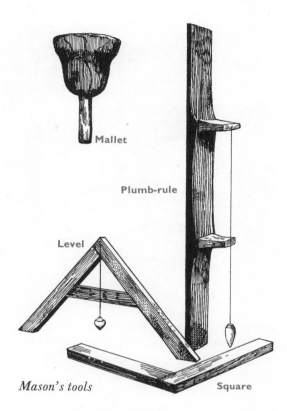

Mason's tools

Mallet

Plumb-rule

Level

Square

a tremendous task, for each of the faces of the Great Pyramid is two hectares in area.

SUMER

The Sumerians used bricks for much of their building. Most soils can be used for making bricks, but those with the greatest clay content give the best results. Water was mixed with the soil and then chopped straw or dung was worked into the mixture. This prevented the bricks from warping or cracking.

The brick-maker had a wooden mould consisting of two brick-sized compartments which he filled with the mixture. He smoothed off the surplus mud and then removed the mould. The bricks were left to dry in the hot sun. The bricks could be made much harder if they were baked in a kiln, but in early times sun-

The ruins of an Assyrian Ramped Temple

dried bricks were mostly used. A more liquid form of the same mixture would be used as mortar or as a plaster for the inside or outside of buildings.

The Sumerians as well as the Egyptians had large public buildings. In the centres of their cities lay a sacred area containing a royal palace and a temple with a high tower or ziggurat as its central feature.

A Ziggurat

The Tower of Babel described in the Book of Genesis was such a tower.

To-day the Middle East is well known for its resources of oil, bitumen and asphalt, and it would be easy to suppose that little use was made of these products until the coming of the motor car. This would be wrong, for bitumen was used in early times to make mastic, a waterproof cement. This had a number of uses. Drains and sewers of brickwork could be waterproofed with this mastic, and in houses bathroom floors could be made waterproof. The Book of Genesis records that the builders of the Tower of Babel ". . . had brick for stone and slime (bitumen) had they for mortar."

The innumerable mixtures and liquids sold to-day to repair pots, pans and other household goods had their counterparts in the mastics of Sumer. Mastics for floors, walls, drains, irrigation channels, ships, and even ploughs were available. The Greeks and Romans however did not use bitumen as much as it was used in Sumer. Soon its use was forgotten.

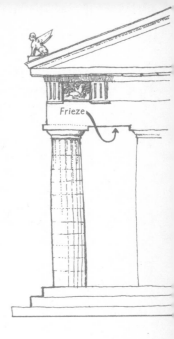

Part of the frieze of the Parthenon

GREECE

Some of the buildings described so far, the pyramids and the ziggurats, are pieces of architecture. Although a building and a piece of architecture both enclose space and provide shelter, the latter has artistic merit as well. Thus a garden shed is a building, whilst a Greek temple is a piece of architecture. The Greeks had large supplies of different types of stone, the best being marble, the most beautiful and monumental of building materials. Theatres, stadia and temples were built in many city states.

In addition to the work they did for public bodies the masons and sculptors produced many works for private buyers. Phidias was one of the great Athenian sculptors and he and his pupils carved a band of marble which ran round the four sides of the Parthenon. You can see the position of this frieze in the diagram and some detail in the photograph.

The blocks of marble used by Greek builders were clamped together by metal fasteners. An almost perfect fit was obtained by grinding the blocks together until the closest contact was achieved. Metal was used in the structure of buildings as well, and iron beams four and a half metres long were used in a temple at Agriento. The Greeks used various wooden devices for moving the large pieces of stone to the building sites, one of which is illustrated below.

Building

ROME

It has been said that the Emperor Augustus (27 B.C. to A.D. 14) "found Rome a city of brick and left it a city of marble." The Romans imported many coloured varieties of marble and used these along with the marble from Carrara to make more colourful buildings than the Greeks. Some idea of the great buildings which existed in Rome can be gained from this reconstruction of the forums of the Emperors.

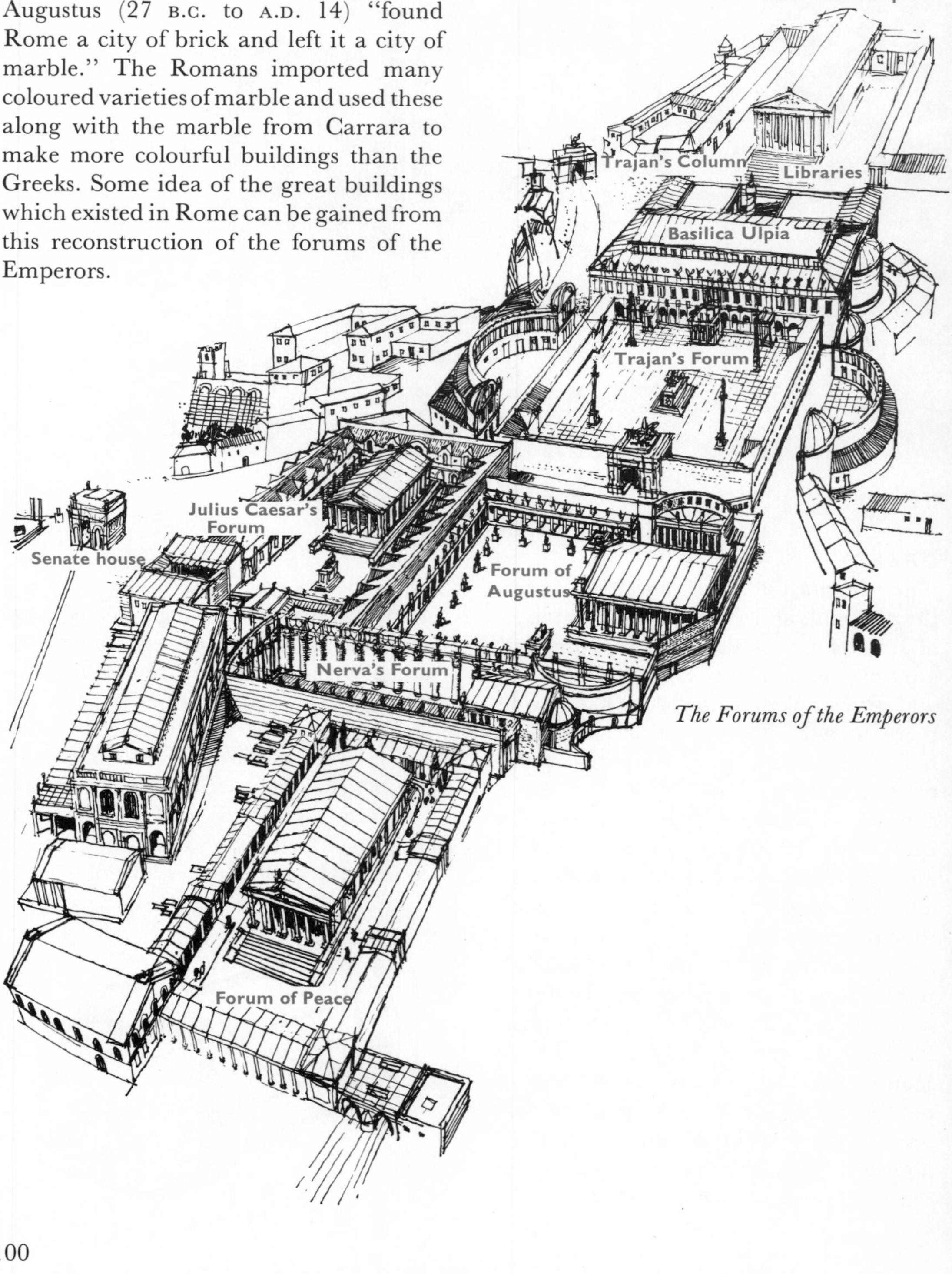

Hadrian's Temple

Trajan's Column

Libraries

Basilica Ulpia

Trajan's Forum

Julius Caesar's Forum

Senate house

Forum of Augustus

Nerva's Forum

The Forums of the Emperors

Forum of Peace

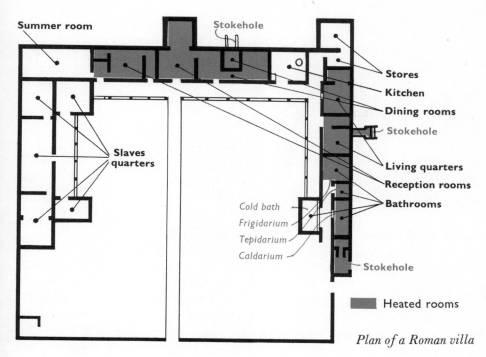

Plan of a Roman villa

Unlike the Greeks, who built with a system of posts and beams, the Romans developed methods of building vaults and domes. A volcanic earth which occurred in the hills near Naples was mixed with lime to form a very strong cement. This was used to make the domes and vaults. The bricks used after the time of Augustus were fired in kilns and lasted much longer than the sun-dried bricks.

One of the remarkable features of some Roman houses, particularly those in the colder parts of the Empire such as Britain, was the hypocaust. This was a system of central heating. A room to be heated by this system was built over a basement between 60cm and 75cm deep. The floor of the room rested on short pillars made of brick or tile. The walls of the room contained flues which enabled the hot air from a nearby furnace to escape after passing under the floor. A diagram of the hypocaust shows the details of its construction.

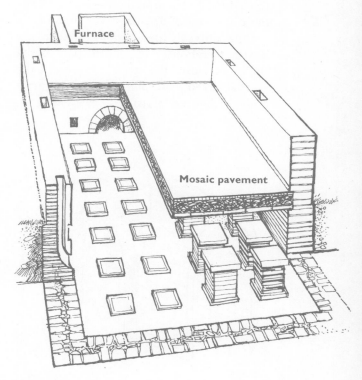

Hypocaust

101

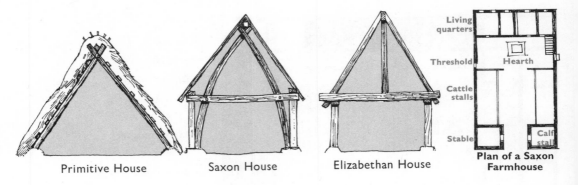

Primitive House   Saxon House   Elizabethan House

Plan of a Saxon Farmhouse

Living quarters

Threshold   Hearth

Cattle stalls

Stable   Calf stall

ANGLO-SAXON ENGLAND

The building of houses in Anglo-Saxon England was based on the primitive cruck house design. Houses before this time had as their main structure two pairs of poles set some distance apart which were linked by a ridge pole. The Saxons refined and added to this simple design as shown in the diagram. Notice in the third diagram that the Elizabethan house still has the main features of its primitive ancestor.

Both animals and people lived in the Saxon farmhouse, the house part being shut off from the part in which the animals lived. The plan of a Saxon farmhouse shows this division.

THE MIDDLE AGES

The buildings which dominated the Middle Ages were the Castle and the Church. Castles are dealt with in the section entitled the Art of War. Early church roofs were often made of wood which easily caught fire. To avoid this risk many Normans built stone vaulted roofs. These roofs were very heavy and the walls had to be very strong to take the weight. If they were not very thick they had to be strengthened with buttresses. Many of the early Norman churches had massive walls and massive stone barrel vaults.

In the years between 1200 and 1500 the

Barrel vault

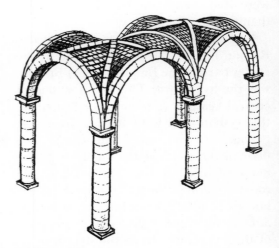

Ribbed vault

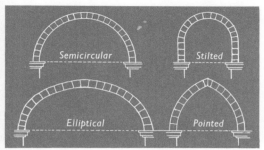

Arches

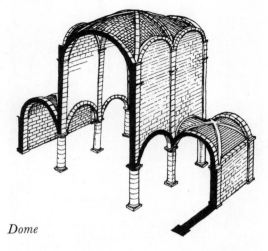

Dome

Gothic style of architecture developed in Europe and the main change was the introduction of the pointed arch.

The magnificent churches of the Middle Ages are a wonderful mixture of beauty and strength. In some cases the builders were more interested in beauty than strength and there were many instances where parts of buildings, or even whole buildings collapsed. The craftsmen who built the original tower at Beverley were described as "not as prudent as they were cunning in their craft; they were concerned rather with beauty than with strength, rather with effect than with the need for safety." In October 1200 this wonderful but hazardous construction fell.

The cathedrals were immense prayers in stone, works of art in which man expressed his deepest feelings in architecture. The designers and builders of these masterpieces were often master masons, or master carpenters; men capable of producing a detailed plan and able to turn this plan into a complete building. These medieval architects knew the qualities of stone, wood, iron and concrete, and in this respect had more practical knowledge than some modern architects. On the other hand they did not possess our present day knowledge of stresses and strains, which might have led them to avoid the mistakes which resulted in the collapse of some of their buildings.

An army of craftsmen and labourers was needed to build a cathedral. Foremost among the craftsmen were the masons who worked the stone and those who placed it in position. The superior branch of masons, the free masons, worked the ashlar. Ashlar was the name given to a rectangular block of stone which had been tooled on the outside face, and which was used in wall building. The second class of masons were called layers, setters or wallers, and they put the worked stones into position. Other masons specialised in the mouldings of arches, window traceries, figure work and images. There were also marblers and polishers who put the finishing touches to the work. Many other craftsmen, among them carpenters, tilers, slaters, thatchers, plumbers, glaziers, smiths and painters, would be required in the course of construction. An unusual craft to be included in this list is the thatcher. He was needed to thatch partly completed walls, and so keep out frost and rain.

The early stages of building were described by Alexander Neckam in 1200:

"Now the ground is made even with the rammer, now the irregularity of the

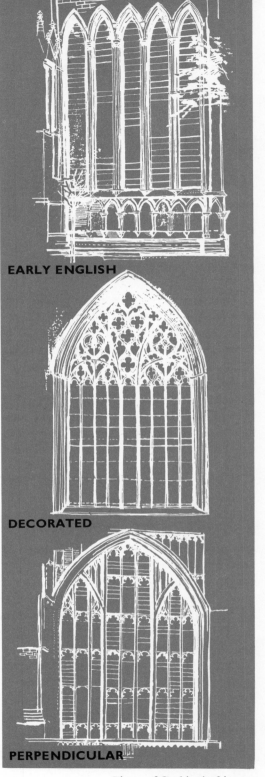

EARLY ENGLISH

DECORATED

PERPENDICULAR

Types of Gothic Architecture

surface is beaten down with frequent ramming, now the solidity of the foundation is tested with piles driven into the bowels of the earth. The height of the wall, built of cut stone and rubble, rises and soars according to the law of the level and the plumbline. The flatness of the surface of the wall is due to the smoothing and polishing of the mason's trowel."

The walls were often topped by a crested parapet. The rain-water ran from the parapet by means of spouts carved into human or animal shapes; these were called gargoyles. The stones were bound together by mortar which was made from a mixture of lime and sand. The lime was produced by burning chalk or limestone in kilns made near to the building site.

When the shell and the roof of the building were complete, the finish of the inside could be considered. The rubble interior of the wall would be plastered and then pointed, and the glaziers would make and put in the beautiful stained glass windows. The variety of finishes was described in Horman's "Vulgaria" in 1519:

"Some men wyll have thys wallys plastered, some pergetted, and whytlymed, some roughe caste, some pricked, some wrought with playster of Paris."

The East window in Carlisle Cathedral in an excellent example of the glazier's craft. The window is sixteen metres high and eight metres wide and the upper part of it consists of eighty-six separate blocks of moulded stone. These are so skilfully made that individual stones can be cut out for repair without endangering the remainder. Many church roofs were covered with silver lead which caused the rain water to run straight off through stone gargoyles.

A Gargoyle—Notre Dame, Paris
Flying Buttresses—Lincoln Cathedral ▲
The East Window, Carlisle Cathedral ▶

Apart from the churches found in towns
and villages there were the monasteries,
which comprised groups of stone buildings
standing in large estates.

Building

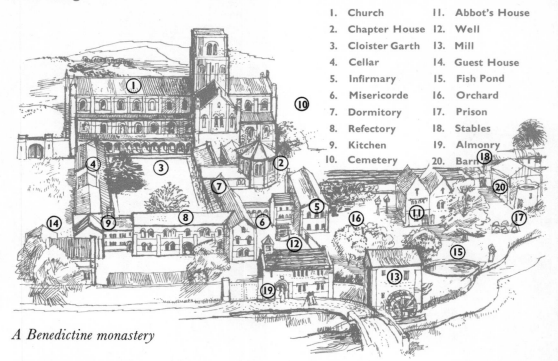

1. Church
2. Chapter House
3. Cloister Garth
4. Cellar
5. Infirmary
6. Misericorde
7. Dormitory
8. Refectory
9. Kitchen
10. Cemetery
11. Abbot's House
12. Well
13. Mill
14. Guest House
15. Fish Pond
16. Orchard
17. Prison
18. Stables
19. Almonry
20. Barn

A Benedictine monastery

TOWN PLANNING

Hippodamus of Miletus is the first known town-planner. He was born about 480 B.C. and he was employed by Pericles the great Athenian statesman to remodel the port of Athens. Hippodamus believed in straight, wide streets and a proper grouping of dwelling houses; this gave his plans a squared effect. Although this sort of planning is orderly it can be monotonous, as is the case with some modern American cities. Some of the towns of the Ancient World had variety and beauty added to planning; such a town was Gerasa in Jordan.

When a town was built in the Ancient World and in the Middle Ages, defence was a major consideration. Hygenus, a Roman architect, considered that a town should not exceed an area of 720 m × 480 m. The reason he gave for this was that longer walls might lead to unclear signals by lookouts, so endangering the town's defences.

Roman towns were built on the chess-board or grid pattern; good examples of this are Turin in N. Italy and Silchester in Britain.

Many people have the impression that towns were not planned in the Middle Ages and that life in them was muddled,

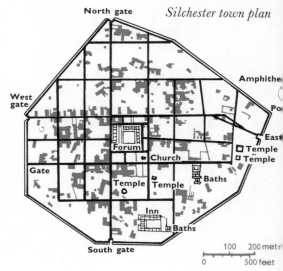

Silchester town plan

106

smelly, yet on occasions colourful. In fact much of the overcrowding in towns took place after the Middle Ages. In Tewkesbury for instance, the long gardens behind the houses on one main road have been built over with rows of cottages, giving a mixture of spacious street design in front and cramped alleys and undersized dwellings behind.

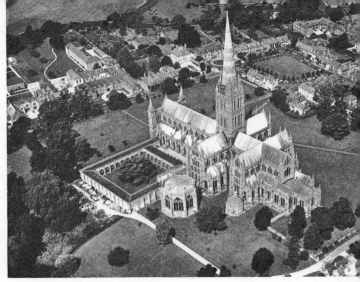

Salisbury Cathedral

Town plans

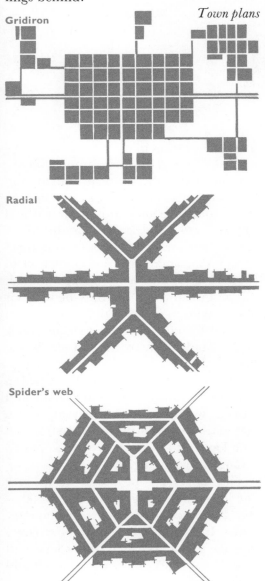

Gridiron

Radial

Spider's web

The opinion that planning has great dangers can be heard in all ages, but careful planning in medieval times produced such beautiful towns as Salisbury with its noble cathedral close. One interesting development in medieval times was the construction of wider rings of fortification as the town increased in size. When the inner fortifications were pulled down the townspeople realised they had the foundations of a circular road, which was of great value to the town. Bologna has a squared plan at the centre and a series of radial roads outside this central area showing clearly this development.

Street plan of Turin

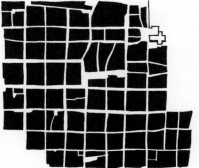

107

Clothing

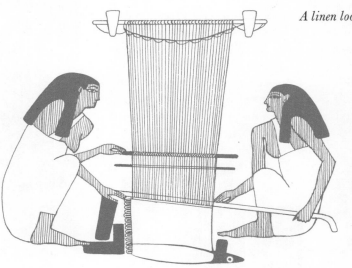

The Ancient World

To combat the cold of the Ice Ages clothing was made of skins sewn together with leather thongs or with strands of sinew. Primitive man used bone or stone scrapers to remove the hair from the skins.

A Bronze Age girl's dress

To make the skin into leather it had to be tanned with fats or other tanning agents. To-day the North American Indians and the Eskimos soften the skins by chewing them, and then they are oil-tanned and smoke-cured. The leather produced by any of these methods will last a long time.

An important discovery was the trick of twisting fibres together to make a thread.

The thread could not only be used for sewing skins to make clothes, but it could be used for bowstrings, for lashing flints to the heads of weapons, and for fishing nets.

The craft of weaving was developed in settled communities. Clothing, mats and baskets were made of different woven materials. In weaving the warp is stretched on a loom and the weft or woof is passed through at right angles.

The Egyptians produced some very fine linen cloths. The tomb of Tutankhamen contained some remarkable tapestry tunics. In Northern Europe wool was used to make garments which were coarse and plain like the girl's dress which was found in Denmark.

A Pharaoh and his Queen

Ionian chiton

Greek himation

Greek tunic

Roman toga

The Greeks and Romans wove much better cloth than was woven in other parts of Europe. Indeed after the fall of the Roman Empire textile crafts declined in Western Europe. After the Norman Conquest textile manufacture began to revive again in England.

However, we must revert to Ancient Greece and the clothing made from the fine woollen cloth. Greek women wore long tunics called chitons while their menfolk wore short-sleeved tunics. In winter, men and women wore wraps known as himations.

The Roman toga was similar to the himation, and in the case of a well-to-do person it was white. Roman women wore a stola which was a form of tunic. In addition, women had a mantle which was worn over the head and shoulders.

Clothing

Roman stolla

By the second century A.D. even workmen wore a licium, a kind of long shirt of linen or wool, which was slipped over the head and fastened round the body with a belt. It reached as far as the knees. The woman's tunic was longer than the man's, and in some cases reached down to the heels. In cold weather people would wear two tunics. Sandals were popular, but in some cases heavy leather boots were worn.

The toga was by custom the most important part of a Roman's dress and it took considerable skill to drape it properly. It took even greater skill to keep the balance of this heavy garment when walking through the jostling crowds of Rome. The Romans were similar to today's housewives in their desire for spotlessly white clothes and many a toga was worn threadbare by repeated washing.

Roman toga

A licium

A Saxon

"They ordeyned and changed every year divers shapes and disguisings of clothing of long large and wide clothes, destitute and desert from all old honeste and good usage; and another time short clothes and tight-waisted, dragged and cut on every side slashed and loose with sleeves and tippets of surcoats and hoods over long and large and overmuch hanging; that they were more like to tormentors and devils than common men; and the women more foolishly surpassed the men in array. . . ."

The Saxon invaders, who settled in Britain after the departure of the Romans, wore sleeved tunics and trousers with puttees and a cloak. The tunics and trousers were made of a material similar to Harris tweed. Hides might be stitched over the cloak to make it more weatherproof.

The greatest change in English costume came in the fourteenth century when English women, particularly the rich, began to discard the conventional garb and wear a wide range of costume. Before this time, for century after century, women wore a kind of nun-like garb not markedly different from that of men. The change in the fourteenth century took place at a time when the influence of the Church was beginning to relax and also when women were no longer being looked upon as mere chattels.

Chaucer blamed the changes on Queen Isabella and Mortimer who de-throned Edward II and brought foreign styles of dress to England. He wrote of the court:

13th century man and woman

Clothing

Regular changes in fashion, the use of expensive materials and jewellery, and even laws confining the use of certain styles to certain ranks of people, made costume a sign of social distinction in the Middle Ages. In fact, some very uncomfortable clothes were worn, but they proclaimed that the wearer was a privileged person and did not have to do heavy work for a living. In the same way, as one writer puts it, "the trailing skirts of the Victorian lady signified that she did not belong to the walking classes."

You will notice in the illustrations of sixteenth century dress that the costumes of the two sexes have parted company. The man could look top heavy in a badly designed garment, but with his legs apart he looks confident, strong and masculine.

14th century costume

The clear waistline on the woman's dress was the major change which made it really feminine.

16th century costume

112

Trade

Phoenician coins

Cretan coins

Greek coins

Roman coins

Early types of money

If you emptied someone's dustbin out on to the ground and sorted over the contents and listed the places where every item had come from, you would certainly find that many parts of the world were represented. The historian does not scorn rubbish heaps, for they can tell him a great deal about the trade that took place in the past. For instance, in the caves of the Dordogne, in Central France, which were occupied at one time by pre-historic men, rubbish heaps have been found which contain the bones of sea-fish and shells. They must have exchanged goods to get these articles.

The advantages of trade have been the same for generations—each community can concentrate on the production of those things it is best able to supply, and by trading its surplus with other communities it can increase the variety of things it enjoys. Trade, though, can only flourish where people trust one another, or where they can work out foolproof methods of exchange. War is the enemy of trade, for it brings destruction and the end of mutual trust. Trade, peace and the exchange of ideas as well as goods, go together and an increase in trade should certainly add to man's comfort.

The development of transport was essential to an increase in trade, and in Egypt, the Nile was the highway for trade. New crafts such as shipbuilding and sail making grew up as sailing boats came into use. Trade was very necessary to the cities of the Tigris-Euphrates delta for even timber and stone had to be imported. A surplus of foodstuffs enabled them to obtain these necessities by exchange.

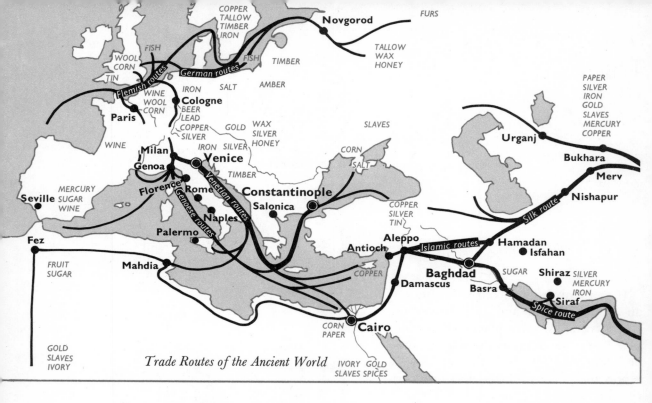

Trade Routes of the Ancient World

The cities of the Indus valley traded with those of the Tigris-Euphrates delta and the markets were similar to a modern Indian bazaar. Among the stalls found in the ruins of these cities were those that sold water. Judging by the large number of shattered cups at Mohenjo-daro each drinker threw his cup away when he had finished, just as we throw away the plastic containers which we use at present day railway buffets. Standardised weights and measures, a common script, good drainage and fine town planning were features of this well ordered and rich civilisation. As in Egypt and the Tigris-Euphrates delta, city life and trade went hand in hand.

The Phoenicians lived on the narrow coastal strip of Syria and became the most famous traders of the Ancient World. Paintings in some Egyptian tombs show the Phoenician traders bartering trinkets with the peasants along the Nile.

Cretan vases have been found in many parts of the Eastern Mediterranean and they give some idea of the extent of trade. One of the main export commodities was probably olive oil, which had a variety of uses in the Ancient World.

Inevitably, the rich cargoes carried by many ships were an attraction, and piracy became a regular occupation for some of the people of the Mediterranean. Fortunately the dangers of a pirate's life are not to every man's liking, and the greater ease and comfort of a steady trade or craft stopped piracy from becoming too widespread.

By the sixth century B.C. the prospects of trade persuaded peasants living near Athens to concentrate on the growing of vines and olive trees instead of merely growing enough food for their own needs. The use of money, particularly small coins, helped trade to take place easily and the produce of the small farmers and the big estates could be exported to increase the wealth and prestige of Athens.

The Greek cities concentrated on trade so much that they depended on other lands for their own supplies. Great Britain was in a similar position in the nineteenth century when she became dependent on supplies of foreign grain. Whatever the risk of a food shortage during war, there is no doubt that both Greeks and British gained a lot of wealth by concentrating on trade.

Once Rome had destroyed Carthage she took control of the trade of the Mediterranean and became a great trading city. There were companies which collected taxes. The collectors were the publicans so often mentioned in the Bible. There were contractors who built roads, bridges and buildings and whose shares were bought and sold on a stock exchange. There were many luxuries to be had and unfortunately prosperity ran to extravagance, and eventually to decay.

Some idea of the trade of the Mediterranean world can be gained from the products which came by land or sea to Rome. There were perfumes, spices, drugs, ivory and jewels from Africa, Arabia and India; gold, furs and forest products from Russia; amber from the Baltic; and metals such as tin and iron from the British Isles and Spain.

As the Roman Empire expanded, the new provinces took up the skills and industries of the Romans and instead of being dependent on Rome soon provided for themselves. In the same way British dominions such as Australia and Canada are now less dependent on British manufactured exports than they used to be. By becoming self-sufficient the Roman provinces contributed to the downfall of the Roman Empire.

The Mediterranean did not cease to be a centre of trading life after the fall of the Roman Empire, and the Roman gold coin, the solidus, was still used in the Dark Ages. With the onset of the Arab invasion in the eighth century A.D., however, the Mediterranean was doomed as a centre of European and Eastern trade. As Ibn Kaldun put it, "The Christians can no longer float a plank on it".

After the success of the first Crusade the Mediterranean was once more open to Western European countries, but the places which gained most were Italian towns such as Venice, Pisa and Genoa. These towns became very prosperous by acting as suppliers to the Crusading armies.

Towns, Markets and Fairs in the Middle Ages

Trade

In the eleventh and twelfth centuries trade increased and towns multiplied. In the same way as farming became the full-time occupation of the landlord and free-holder on the manor, trade became the full-time occupation of the merchant and craftsman in the town. Medieval towns were like little islands of freedom in a feudal sea, and whilst fairs were on even fugitive serfs could not be arrested.

Many towns were set up in good defensive positions, or at fording places by rivers. They provided safe and convenient sites for trading. The town wall was doubly useful for it afforded a good defence in war and in peacetime it ensured that traders entered by the gates and paid the toll charged to those who wished to trade in the market place.

Markets were generally held each week, but fairs took place each year and were much more lavish affairs, attracting traders from distant parts. The Stourbridge Fair, which was held near Cambridge, lasted until the eighteenth century and attracted traders from all over Europe.

The international trade fairs like the Leipzig Fair are the last echo of the Medieval fairs. All that remains of the local fairs are the merry-go-rounds and side shows; the trade has gone, but the merriment has stayed on.

Many of the early English towns were on the royal demesne. This was no accident, for the English kings were more likely than any other landlord to grant a charter for a town to govern itself. Kings were often short of money and

A street in a Medieval town

116

Officer of a Craft Guild

WARDEN

SEARCHERS

Freemen of
the Guild

MASTERS

JOURNEYMEN

APPRENTICES

Diagram of guild organisation

charged large sums for the grant of a charter. A charter might be granted for only a limited period so that the king had the opportunity to make more money when the date for renewal came round.

The control of trade, and the buying and selling of goods, was in the hands of the Merchant Guilds. Later when town industries grew up each separate craft had its operations governed by a Craft Guild. The Merchant Guild made sure that customer and seller got a fair deal and punished those responsible for sharp practice. Craft Guilds, too, aimed at making sure that maker and purchaser were fairly treated. The diagram shows you how a Craft Guild was organised and on page 118 you can see the typical craftsman's establishment where goods were made and sold; a miniature factory and shop combined.

The work of the guild officials was made easier by having all the shops of one trade in one street.

Both Merchant and Craft Guilds had schemes to help their members in distress, just in the way that we insure against unemployment and ill-health today. Those who produced poor quality goods, such as a swordsmith who soldered a broken sword together and sold it as new, would be heavily punished, for they brought disgrace on their craft.

Apprentices, or learners, had to spend many years, seven or more, learning their trade and as their apprenticeship document shows, master and apprentice had many duties towards each other.

England's most important products in the Middle Ages were wool and woollen cloth. Like the town charter, these were possible sources of money for the King. Edward III's policy in the fourteenth century was to foster the industry by

A craftsman's establishment

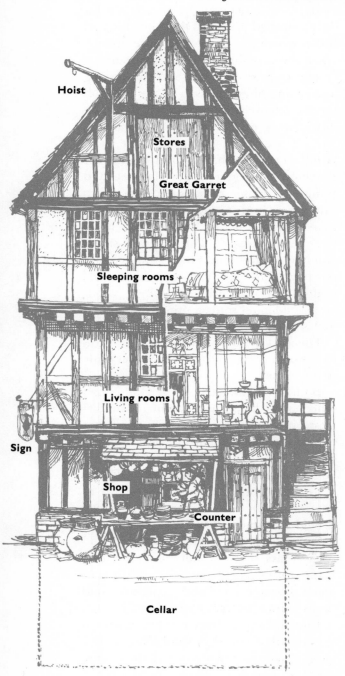

Hoist

Stores

Great Garret

Sleeping rooms

Living rooms

Sign

Shop

Counter

Cellar

attracting foreign craftsmen, particularly Flemish weavers, and by prohibiting the export of raw wool. Foreign cloth was barred from entering England in 1337 and with this tight royal control the woollen industry began to grow so that by 1500 the Merchant Adventurers Company exported 60 000 cloths.

Cloth is a good subject with which to end this section, for one piece of good Flemish cloth is in itself almost the story of medieval trade. This cloth, woven in Flanders from English wool, coloured by red dyes from the Mediterranean, or by madder or woad from North-West Europe, giving reds and blues respectively. Potash from the Baltic was used in the dyeing process. When fulling or shrinking was done in the fulling mill, fuller's earth from England or France was used. Lastly, the teasels for raising the nap on the cloth came from England. This piece of Flemish cloth was indeed a product of European trade.

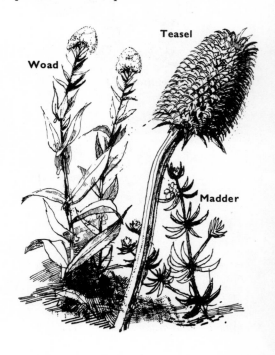

Woad

Teasel

Madder

Power

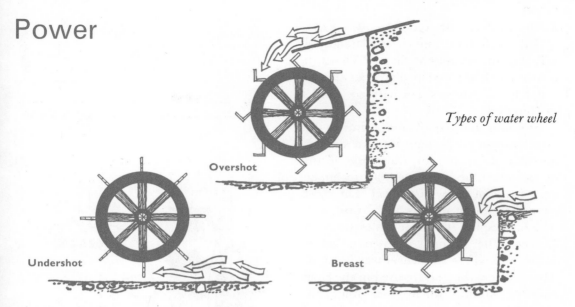

Types of water wheel

Overshot

Undershot

Breast

POWER IN THE ANCIENT WORLD

The three types of power used before the introduction of steam in the eighteenth century were animal, water and wind. In Rome for some time, the most common forms of power used were men, in the form of slaves, and animals. Gangs of slaves pulled the heavy blocks which made the pyramids, and galley slaves provided the power for Greek and Roman ships which sailed the Mediterranean Sea.

It seems strange that harnessed animals were not used to replace human labour. A study of the types of harness used in the Ancient World shows that apart from the ox with its appropriate yoke no other beast had a harness which enabled it to pull heavy loads. The types of harness used for horses, donkeys or asses merely choked them when they began to pull even a moderate load. Therefore these animals were used either for riding, or as pack animals. It was not until the Middle Ages that a satisfactory collar harness was made and the horse then began to displace the ox in drawing ploughs, carts and other vehicles.

In countries such as Spain where the land is dry and dusty horses can go unshod, but in Northern Europe the hoof of a horse quickly became worn and damaged. Clearly until a satisfactory nailed shoe was developed horses could not be used to the best advantage in Northern Europe.

Medieval cart showing collar harness

By the ninth century there is evidence of a nailed horseshoe, and in the reign of Edward the Confessor in the eleventh century we know that he placed an annual order for 120 horseshoes with six smiths in Hereford.

A serious shortage of labour during the later years of the Roman Empire made it necessary to search for alternative forms of power. One solution was to make greater use of the water wheel. The most primitive water mill is the Norse mill which, despite its name, was used in Greece. The Romans devised a better water mill where the wheel was upright. These water wheels were used in the corn mills of Rome, Athens and other big cities.

Norse mill

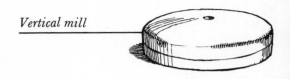

Vertical mill

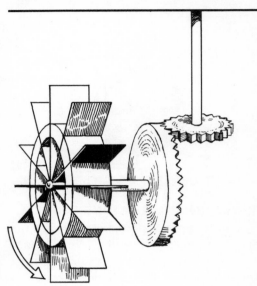

There are three main types of water wheel, the undershot, the overshot and the breast. The first of these only worked effectively in swiftly flowing streams or rivers with a constant volume of water. The overshot was found to be more efficient. This was operated by water which came through a sluice to a mill-race and chute set in such a way that the water hit the wheel forcing it to turn round. The most efficient, and the least used in the Ancient World, was the breast water wheel.

At Barbegal in France the Romans built a flour factory which had its mill stones driven by two sets of eight overshot water wheels. These mills could turn out nearly three tonnes of flour in a ten-hour day. The conduits received their water from an aqueduct, and you can see in the plan how the wheels were arranged.

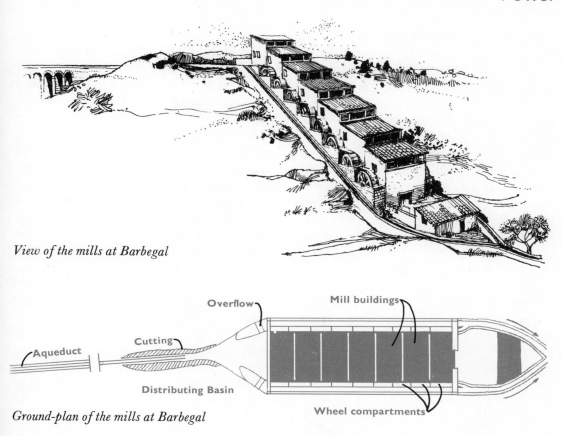

View of the mills at Barbegal

Overflow

Mill buildings

Cutting

Aqueduct

Distributing Basin

Wheel compartments

Ground-plan of the mills at Barbegal

One interesting development was the floating mill. The mills were placed on firmly anchored boats and the force of the water rotated the mill wheels. Boat mills of this type were used by the Venetians and the French in the Middle Ages.

Floating mill

POWER IN THE MIDDLE AGES

The uses of the water mill were extended a great deal in the Middle Ages. It was used not only for grinding corn but for raising water, pressing oil seeds, grinding, fulling, papermaking, tanning and for moving such tools as hammers, saws and lathes. The Domesday Book records the presence of 5624 water mills in England in 1086.

The development of the fulling mill had important effects on the English woollen industry. In the process of fulling the cloth was beaten with wooden mallets so that the fibres in the cloth were more closely knit together. The mallets were driven by the water wheels. In the later Middle Ages the woollen industry moved

121

away from the cities, often to remote up-land valleys where the fulling mills could be operated effectively by the fast-flowing streams. Water power became essential to mining and the production of metals, for it was used to drain mines and to work the bellows and hammers used in the forges.

The power of the wind was harnessed by the windmills which became a common feature of the windy coasts of N.W. Europe in the Middle Ages. The earliest known definite mention of a windmill is in a twelfth century deed, and it is certain that the development of the windmill is an achievement of craftsmen of the Middle Ages.

The Post Mill

The post mill worked on the principle that the mill sails would offer resistance to the wind which would turn them round. The mill house was mounted on an upright

A post mill

post and could be turned through a full circle so that the mill sails could be faced to the wind when necessary. When the mill was not working the sails of canvas could be rolled up on the wooden lattice work.

The construction and operation of a fifteenth century post mill is a good illustration of the skill of the millwright. The central post had to be strong and secure, and so the millwright made sure that it was braced thoroughly as shown in the diagram. This lower part of the mill was surrounded by a roundhouse which with the bracing struts and central post made a strong base to the mill. The mill-stones were placed so that their weight was evenly spread.

When the miller wished to start the mill he would have to turn the millhouse into the wind. One of his men would pull the ladder clear of the ground and then attach the ring at the end of a chain round one of the small posts shown in the diagram. He would wind up the chain and so pull the mill closer to a post. He would continue until the millhouse was pulled into the wind. The next step would be to shut the louvres, or openings in the sails, so that the mill-sails offered resistance to the wind. With the mill-sails going round the miller could begin to grind his corn.

The gearwheels in the mill were made mostly of pear wood. This wood is hard and oily, and will therefore stand a great deal of wear. The grain ran down chutes to the holes in the centres of the grind-stones. The flour came out at the sides of the stones and then fell into other chutes and finally into bins or sacks.

Considerable effort was needed to pull the millhouse of a post mill into the wind and towards the end of the Middle Ages the tower mill began to take its place.

The parts of a windmill

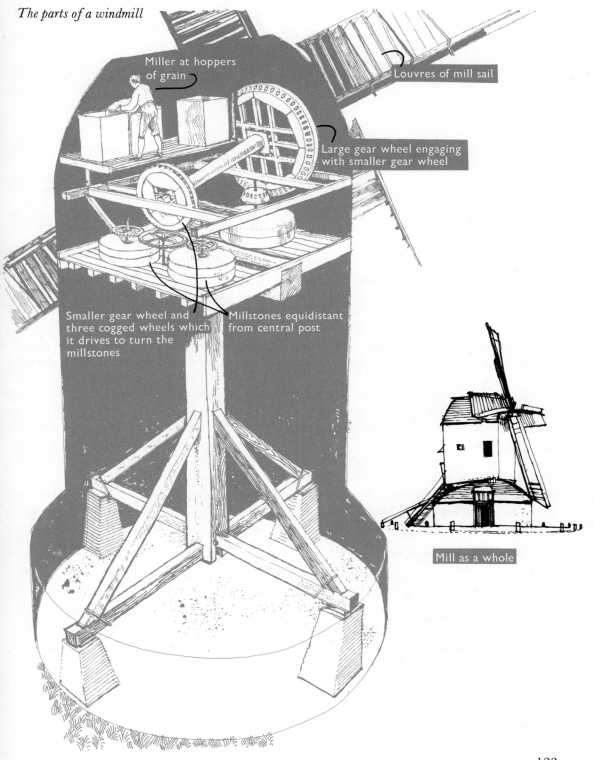

Miller at hoppers of grain

Louvres of mill sail

Large gear wheel engaging with smaller gear wheel

Smaller gear wheel and three cogged wheels which it drives to turn the millstones

Millstones equidistant from central post

Mill as a whole

Transport by Land and Sea

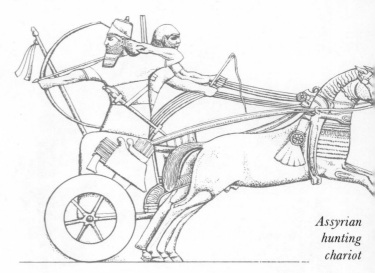

Assyrian hunting chariot

TRANSPORT BY LAND

Before animals were tamed, man's most reliable beast of burden was woman. The ass was possibly the first pack animal, whilst its relative, the onager, was harnessed to a vehicle in Mesopotamia before 3000 B.C. Oxen were mainly used for pulling ploughs or carts. The horse was largely used in war.

The first land vehicles were sledges. Originally they were nothing more than hollowed-out tree trunks, which could be used to drag a kill back to the cave or shelter where the hunter lived. Runners were later put on to sledges and, understandably, quite a few examples of these have been found in North European countries where they could be dragged easily over the winter snow.

The earliest type of wheel was made of three pieces of wood clamped together by wooden struts. The royal tombs at Ur contained wheeled vehicles, the rims of which were studded with copper nails. These nails may have been used to fasten leather tyres to the wheels. It is unlikely that the carts could have been used for much more than carrying foodstuffs from the fields to village or town, and carrying manure in the opposite direction, for good roads and bridges were rare before Roman times.

Solid wheels were strong and lasted a long time, but they were heavy and clumsy and not much good for fast trans-

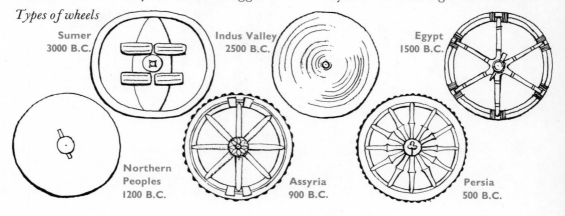

Types of wheels

Sumer 3000 B.C.

Indus Valley 2500 B.C.

Egypt 1500 B.C.

Northern Peoples 1200 B.C.

Assyria 900 B.C.

Persia 500 B.C.

124

Egyptian wheelwrights

port. Spoked wheels were used in Egypt soon after 1600 B.C., and you can see Egyptian wheelwrights at work in the illustration. The wheels probably turned freely on the axles. The early carts were easy to dismantle, this being an advantage when obstacles such as rivers or swampy places had to be crossed. Oxen, yoked in pairs on either side of a single shaft, were used to pull the carts.

The Sumerians used onagers to draw their war chariots, but other peoples such as the Hittites used horse-drawn chariots with spoked wheels. The development of chariots with spoked wheels soon led to the improvement of roads. Trackways existed in Egypt and in Crete, but the most skilled road builders of ancient times were the Romans. The first of the great Roman highways was the Appian Way, which was begun in 312 B.C. It was 260 kilometres long. The safety of the Roman Empire depended on its roads.

A surveyor was responsible for the lay-out of roads and cities. He was accompanied by his assistants who carried a groma and a number of rods. The groma consisted of a staff with a cross at the top from the ends of which hung small weights on cords. The groma would be set up (see page 126) and the surveyor would send his assistants with the rods to determine roughly the position where a wall or road was to be built. Once in position he could, by asking them to move a little, get cords and rods in one straight line.

Sumerian four-wheeled war chariots

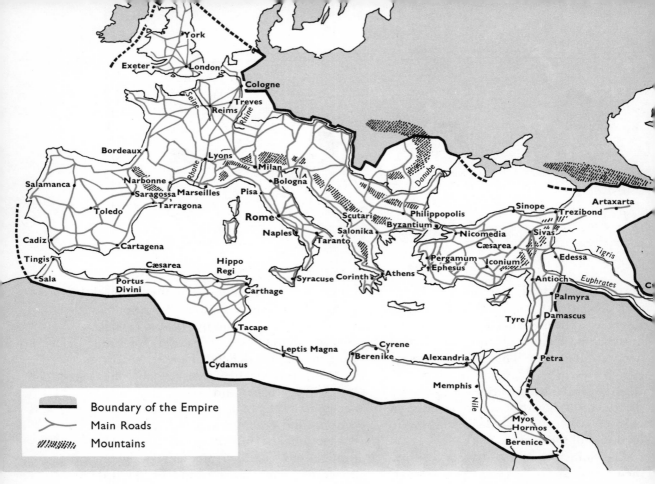

The main roads of the Roman Empire

Roman surveyor using a groma

The system of Roman roads made communication between the central government and the provinces efficient. The horses which were used by official couriers were changed regularly at post stations at intervals of about six to sixteen Roman miles.

The roads were only fully paved where there was a lot of traffic, such as in towns and on their outskirts. Most other roads had a gravel surface which, if looked at in cross-section, was higher in the middle than at the sides. This is termed cambering, and ensures that the rain runs off into the ditches at the sides of the road.

126

Stone setts
Concrete with crushed stone
Slabs in cement
Mortar
Sand

Cross-section of a Roman road

Along with the roads the Romans constructed fine bridges of timber and of stone. Both the Thames and the Danube were spanned by timber or half timber bridges, but the remains of some surviving Roman bridges indicate that they were often built of stone and cement.

One of the worst results of the fall of the Roman Empire was the breakdown of a central government which gave an important place to public works such as roads. During and after the Middle Ages the people of Europe relied on what was left of the Roman system of roads. When

Roman bridge at Alcantara

new roads were built in the Middle Ages cobbles and broken stones were used in their construction.

The two-wheeled and four-wheeled carts of the Middle Ages were similar to those of ancient times except for the addition of shafts such as those shown in the drawing below.

A two-wheeled cart

TRANSPORT BY SEA

Early man used whatever was convenient to help him to keep afloat: in Egypt bundles of rushes, in other places wooden logs. Eventually a true boat was produced in which hollowness gave buoyancy and better protection to the boatmen.

The Egyptians needed some device to strengthen their plank-built boats which had no keels. [Imagine your body without a spine and you have some idea of the problem which faced the Egyptian boat builder.] They eventually overcame this weakness by what was known as a hogging truss—a cable running from bow to stern which was supported on wooden crutches as shown below.

The types of ships used in the Mediterranean were based upon the dug-out. Some boats still have a hollowed keel and it seems reasonable to suppose that boat builders in ancient times added ribs and planks to the dug-out keel and produced the sort of structure which we would recognise as a boat. The Greeks produced Biremes, Triremes and Quinqueremes, though it is not certain whether these terms referred to the number of banks of oars, or the number of men employed on each oar. The design and use of these warships is dealt with in the Art of War Section.

A coracle

A reed boat

A quaffa

An Egyptian sea-going boat

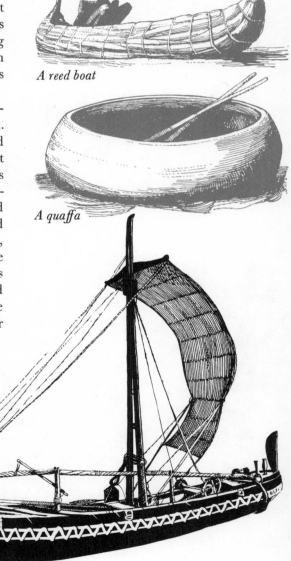

A war galley

A Phoenician ship

These early ships often hugged the coasts of the Mediterranean, but even so by 1500 B.C. men were sailing directly from Crete to Egypt.

The wars between Rome and Carthage led the Romans to construct a navy and their victory brought them control of the Mediterranean. By the reign of Caligula the Roman shipbuilders had mastered the art of building large ships, larger than any wooden ship of the line at the time of the Crimean War eighteen hundred years later. Mussolini ordered Lake Nemi to be drained in the twentieth century so that the remains of these pleasure ships could be studied. These ships were not typical of those built by the Romans. They were another instance of the urge to display by emperors such as Caligula. The Roman merchant ships look low in the bow and high in the stern; this was because they were designed for running before the wind rather than struggling against it. Even in Elizabethan times ships were still built in this way, but this construction would be a disadvantage when beating against the sea and wind.

Ships of the Ancient World were steered by a large oar attached to the stern. For river and coastal sailing and for most voyages in the Mediterranean Sea this method was quite adequate.

The rudder, which was much more effective than the steering oar, was developed in the Middle Ages.

A Roman merchant ship

An early Greek ship

J

The Vikings

The custom amongst the Norsemen of burial in ships has resulted in the preservation of some of their boats. One such boat was found at Gokstad in Norway. It was 23·4 m long and 5·03 m in the beam. These vessels were light and buoyant with a square sail on a single mast set amidships. Sixteen oarsmen on each side could be used to propel the boat when this was necessary.

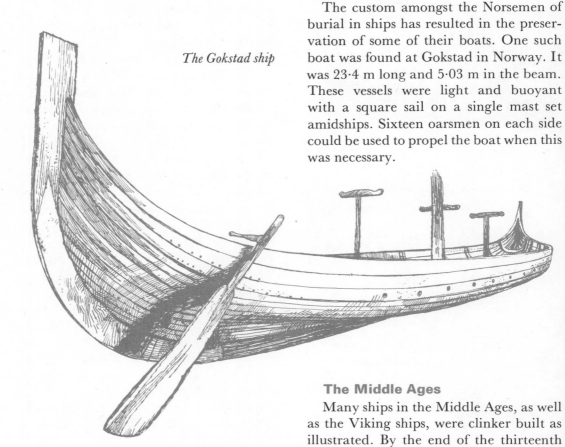

The Gokstad ship

The Middle Ages

Many ships in the Middle Ages, as well as the Viking ships, were clinker built as illustrated. By the end of the thirteenth century the stern-post rudder was in use.

Stern-post rudder

Clinker built

The Tree-nails T pass through three thicknesses of wood whilst the iron bolts B hold five thicknesses of wood together

130

Gradually the number of sails and masts on merchant ships was increased and by the fifteenth century three-masted ships with a forecastle and aftercastle were at sea. You can see the names of the various parts of the ship below.

The ship of the later Middle Ages could make use of almost any wind; it did not have to wait for a favourable one as Roman merchant ships had to do many centuries earlier.

The introduction of the magnetic compass ends the story of the ship before the discoveries of the fifteenth and sixteenth centuries.

Parts of a ship

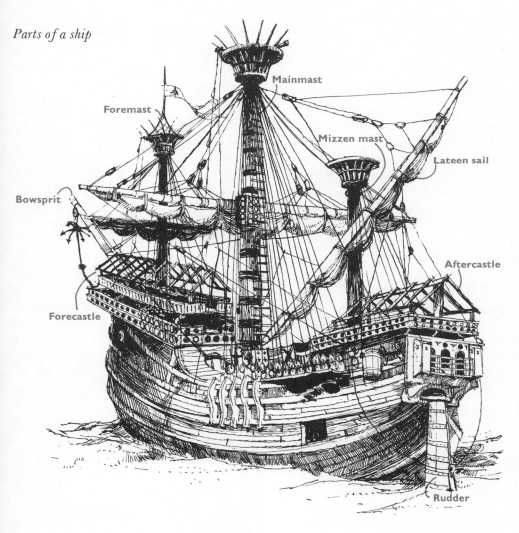

- Mainmast
- Foremast
- Mizzen mast
- Lateen sail
- Bowsprit
- Aftercastle
- Forecastle
- Rudder

The Art of War

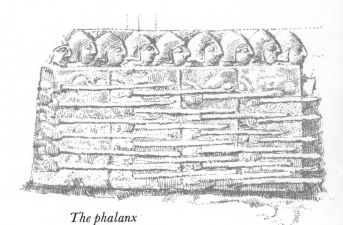

The phalanx

The earliest farmers on the earth had plenty of land and so far as we know they were peaceful people. Later, though, due to wasteful methods of farming and the habit of moving from place to place, men would fight for possession of the best land. Wars have often been caused by disputes over land, and so-called religious wars such as the Crusades were in part caused by the desire of some Crusading knights to own estates in the Holy Land.

WAR ON LAND

In Ancient Times

The people of the New Stone Age with earthen walls and wooden stockades around their settlements, clearly had their wars, so too did the Egyptians who under the Pharaohs developed armies of charioteers and archers. It was in Sumer, though, that the art of war was developed most in early times. The Sumerian war chariots are the earliest known wheeled vehicles. Apart from his war chariots, the king of a Sumerian city had his men grouped in one massive fighting unit called a phalanx. They were well disciplined as you can see from the illustrations, and were armed with spears and protected by a wall of tall shields.

About 2500 B.C. the region of Akkad, in the northern part of the plain of Shinar, was ruled by Sargon, the first ruler to use war to gain himself an Empire. Centuries later the Assyrians conquered a large area of the Middle East, and wherever they went they left ruin.

The Assyrians were the first people to have whole armies with weapons of iron. They had skilled cavalry and charioteers and their foot soldiers were made up of archers, spearmen and shield bearers. In addition they used the battering ram and siege machinery. The walls of cities which they attacked were often made of sun-dried brick which could not stand up to a pounding by the Assyrian battering rams. The loot from their victims helped towards the upkeep of the armies.

One of the greatest problems was to supply an army with fresh water. Wells were dug in the dry bed of the river during one war, while during another against the Arabs, the king, Ashur-bani-pal, set guards on all wells and boasted, "I made drink costly to their mouths; through thirst and deprivation they perished."

The citizen-soldiers of Athens proved the effectiveness of the spear at the battle of Marathon, but it was at sea where the Greeks made great changes in the methods of fighting. It was to the north of Greece, in Macedonia, that the next advance in land warfare was made.

Philip of Macedon, father of Alexander the Great, made a permanent, or standing army of full-time soldiers. These men were armed with spears and were formed into a larger phalanx than had ever been used before in war. Philip was fortunate in that his kingdom possessed plenty of horses. His nobles were used to fighting on horseback, and Philip drilled them to attack as a mass. This massed cavalry charge could win battles, and kept its place in land warfare for centuries.

The third change Philip made concerned the whole army, for it worked as one unit directed by Philip, with the phalanx in the centre and the forces of cavalry on the wings.

Alexander's army for the invasion of Asia numbered about 40 000 men. He had 5000 cavalry and the remainder were infantry of various types, including engineers who surveyed roads, built bridges and constructed and operated siege weapons. The phalanx contained 9000 men who were organised into six battalions of 1500 men each. Alexander was fortunate in taking over the fine army that his father had prepared, but the use he made of it showed him to be an outstanding commander. He was far-sighted and able to seize opportunities in the midst of battle. Also he had tremendous drive, and without these qualities he could not have marched his army across to India.

One example of Alexander's careful attention to his army was his establish-

A Greek hoplite

ment of a field post office. This pleased his troops, for they were able to write home. It was useful to Alexander, for he was able to have the letters secretly censored and keep a check on the morale of his army.

The Roman Army

The Roman army was one of the most efficient and long-lived armies in history, and the willingness of Romans to accept discipline was the basis of this great army. A Roman Legion contained between 3000 and 6000 infantry and a cavalry unit of 300 horsemen. Command was in the hands of the Lieutenant of the Legion who was assisted by officers known as military tribunes. Centurians commanded units of roughly 100 men each and were the equivalent of senior N.C.O.'s in modern armies.

133

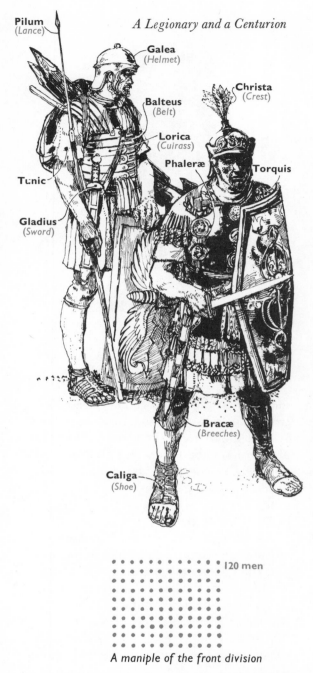

A Legionary and a Centurion

Pilum (Lance)

Galea (Helmet)

Christa (Crest)

Balteus (Belt)

Lorica (Cuirass)

Phaleræ

Torquis

Tunic

Gladius (Sword)

Bracæ (Breeches)

Caliga (Shoe)

120 men

A maniple of the front division

The dress and weapons of a legionary are shown in the illustration. When on the march, the Roman soldier would carry a twenty kilogramme pack which contained clothing, entrenching tools, two stakes—his contribution to a camp pallisade—a handmill for grinding wheat, rations and cooking pots. Each Legion had a standard carried by a standard bearer who wore a leopard skin.

The Romans did not in general admire war, they understood it. The Roman line of battle shown in the diagram below was a great improvement. The Legion was divided into three lines; the front line contained the young and vigorous troops whilst the older and more experienced troops were put in the other two lines. The maniples of each line were arranged so that between each maniple there was a space as wide as the maniple of the second line. Notice that in the diagram the maniples of the second line cover the spaces between the maniples of the front line and, as you would anticipate, the maniples of the third line cover the spaces between those of the second line.

This formation had many advantages, for instance the first and second lines could close up to present a solid front or the swordsmen of the first and second lines could retire between the maniples of the third line to gain some rest. Good discipline meant that the Roman generals could control their troops throughout a battle and take advantage of their opponents' mistakes.

Roman threefold line of battle

Rear Division

Middle Division

Front Division

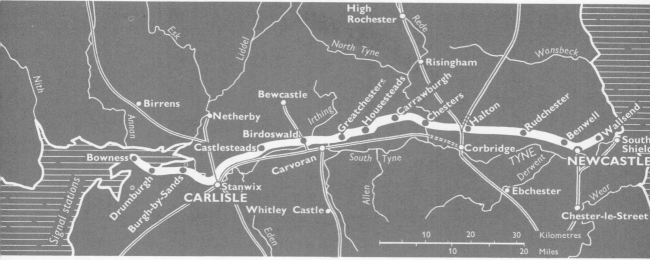

Hadrian's Wall and its outposts

Whenever a Roman army rested it built a fortified camp. The men would build a ridge of earth around the camp and drive the wooden posts which they carried into the top of this ridge. Permanent military occupation led emperors such as Hadrian to take an engineer's view of defence.

Where good natural barriers did not exist, or had to be added to, the Roman engineers planned defensive lines. One of the most impressive was Hadrian's Wall, between the mouth of the River Tyne and Solway Firth. The wall was seventy-six Roman miles long and at intervals along the wall were mile castles, manned by fighting garrisons. If an attack took place the Romans went through one of the wide sally-ports in the wall and encircled their opponents and drove them against the wall.

Discipline was kept by quite severe punishments on occasions. Cowardice or mutiny could result in decimation, the execution of one man in every ten, while minor offences were punished by short rations, pack drill or flogging.

WAR AT SEA

In the Ancient World

The Athenian fleet played a vital part in the victory of the Greeks over the Persians. The Piræus was the biggest dockyard in Greece and it must have been a marvellous experience for a Greek boy to see the ships being built, and to be told of the tactics the Athenian sailors developed to defeat their opponents. Normally fighting at sea in the Ancient World and as late as the fifteenth century was a matter of fighting a land battle at sea. The sailors had the job of laying their ships alongside those of their enemies so that the troops could board the other ships.

The Athenians developed methods of fighting which made them masters of the Eastern Mediterranean. The prows of their ships were specially constructed so that they could withstand the impact of hitting another ship. Furthermore this prow was swept forward with a strong ram below the waterline. It was no longer a matter of laying the ship alongside the enemy, but of hitting the enemy as hard

135

A Greek trireme

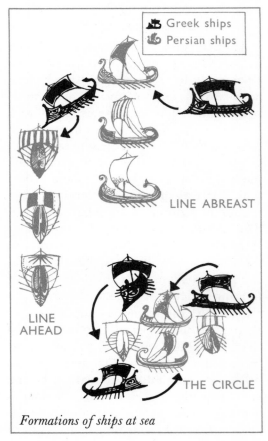

Formations of ships at sea

as possible amidships and then back paddling and leaving the sea to do the rest.

Various defensive measures were taken against ramming; these included the formation of a line or a circle of ships. The Athenians found a counter to both of these measures. They rowed around a line of ships and attacked the sterns. In the case of a circle they sailed in ever decreasing circles round their opponents until the enemy's oars locked. Then they attempted to break for the open sea. Once this happened the Athenians were presented with a number of easy targets for ramming.

The Romans relied entirely on boarding to win their battles at sea and to help them in this task they built hinged gangways with spikes on the outer ends. The gangway was kept raised until alongside an enemy ship, then it was let go to pierce the deck and provide a boarding bridge for the soldiers. Only with the development of naval guns did war at sea become basically different from war on land.

136

WAR ON LAND AND SEA AFTER THE FALL OF THE ROMAN EMPIRE

Most people have seen pictures of armed knights mounted on powerful horses charging towards their enemies, but few will realise either how long it took before the mounted knight became really useful, or the part played by each piece of equipment worn by rider and horse. Imagine trying to control a horse without the stirrup and to fight with a spear that was no more than a blade attached to a wooden shaft. Even if you kept your seat you would be unable to retract your spear from your opponent.

Two important developments took place in the period after the fall of the Roman Empire. First, the saddle replaced the horse blanket, and second, the heavy horse, ancestor of the destrier, appeared.

The saddle gave support front and back to the rider with the pommel and cantle, while the stirrup gave central support.

By the first part of the eighth century A.D. the stirrup was in use in Europe and it is likely that it was introduced from Asia.

A knight on horseback

Mongol horsemen

The Franks developed the wing spear in the eighth century and the spurs below the blade had the same function as the horsetail behind the blade of Mongol spears. Spur or horsetail prevented deep penetration in the flesh of an enemy and thereby gave the rider a chance to retain his weapon in shock combat.

As in the case of the fighter aircraft with fixed guns, the knight on his destrier aimed his horse at his opponent. He held his lance between the upper arm and the body and delivered the blow not with his muscles but with the weight of himself and his charging horse. Shock cavalry were the key units in warfare until the longbow began to threaten the cavalryman in the later Middle Ages.

Piracy was the profession of the Vikings and like most professionals they were very efficient. They attacked with tremendous speed. Each longboat had sixteen oars and contained forty fighting men. Apart from being strong enough to sail the open sea, the longships were excellent for sailing up navigable rivers

and were easy to beach and carry overland.

When the Vikings landed they often rounded up all the horses they could find and moved swiftly to the object of their attack, often a monastery or church which they would strip of its valuables. The surprise and speed of their raids bred a hopeless misery in many parts of Europe until Alfred and the men of Wessex gave effective resistance to the Northmen.

In 1066 the English used the double-headed axe and the "shield wall" against the Normans. Armour made of chain mail was worn by most of the Normans and by some of Harald's men. Lance, spear, sword and bow were the main weapons in the eleventh century and they remained so until the end of the Middle Ages. There were changes however in tactics, armour and the weapons themselves. As the longbow came into general use so the English in particular used bodies of archers to break up defensive infantry formations and charges by mounted knights.

A shield wall

The battle of Crécy, 1346, one of the great victories won by the English in the Hundred Years' War, is a good example of the important part the archer played in warfare in the Middle Ages. The campaigns in Scotland had taught the English new tactics which they employed at Crécy.

Before the battle was fought, the archers protected their positions in two ways by digging holes and driving iron-shod stakes firmly into the earth. The French made fifteen attacks on the English position and each time suffered very heavy losses from the fire of the English longbowmen. The French were finished off by dismounted English men-at-arms. Note on the diagram the way in which the archers have been positioned in the English line of battle.

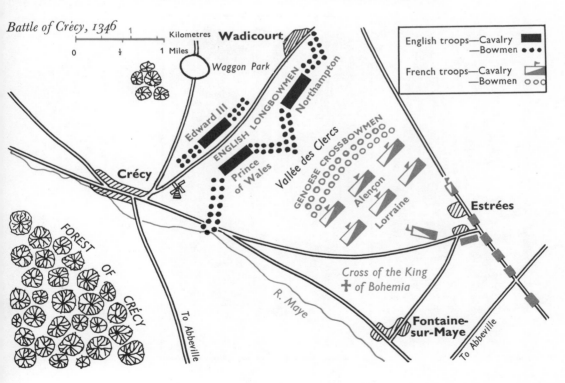

Battle of Crécy, 1346

Kilometres

Wadicourt

Waggon Park

English troops—Cavalry
—Bowmen

French troops—Cavalry
—Bowmen

Edward III

ENGLISH LONGBOWMEN

Northampton

Prince of Wales

Vallée des Clercs

GENOESE CROSSBOWMEN

Crécy

Alençon

Lorraine

Estrées

FOREST OF CRÉCY

Cross of the King
✝ of Bohemia

R. Maye

To Abbeville

Fontaine-sur-Maye

To Abbeville

139

A Siege

See if you can piece together all the activities of a siege force from the following illustrations.

Digging trenches for a sap

Constructing a siege tower

Hurdles to protect the archers

Scaling ladders

A castle under siege

Devices for hurling stones

The Arts

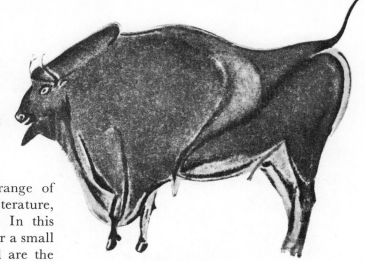

A cave painting

"The Arts" cover a wide range of human activity. They include literature, music, painting and sculpture. In this section it is only possible to cover a small part of the arts. Those selected are the ones that can be illustrated. Together with the illustrations of paintings, sculpture, pottery and musical instruments is a commentary which should help you to understand how these arts have developed through the ages.

Many people, children and adults, will complain that, "I don't like classical music," or "I don't like modern art". Often they have made little attempt to understand the arts. Some knowledge of the history of the arts should help you to enjoy them.

PREHISTORIC ART

In many parts of the world paintings on rock surfaces and in caves, and pieces of sculpture in bone, ivory or stone, have been found. The paintings found deep in caves in France and Spain show animals and hunting scenes, and it is possible that these caves were ceremonial centres. The earlier pottery and stone structures made by men were crude and undecorated. Later they were well designed.

Neolithic pottery and flint instruments

141

Stonehenge, Wiltshire

An Egyptian mummy

New Stone Age people erected structures such as Stonehenge.

PRE-CLASSICAL TIMES

In Ancient Egypt there was a very close link between art and religious belief. The Egyptians believed in an after life and made special provision for the dead in the tombs. The dead body was mummified to preserve it, but in case the mummy suffered damage or gradually broke up, stone statues were placed in the tomb. These statues could be the resting place of the spirit if a mummy was destroyed. The spirit had to be fed, and if the Egyptians could believe that a spirit would live in a statue, then they could easily believe that all the necessities of life could be provided in the form of carvings. Thus a tomb became a picture book of Egyptian life. Many of the Egyptian stone figures are of the standing or walking type, an indication that Egyptian craftsmen kept to a traditional style in sculpture, as they did in painting and relief work.

Mesopotamian art is as old as that of Egypt. The theme of this art, especially that of Assyria, is war and conquest. Lions and bulls with human heads appear in much of this work. Much of it is skilful, but the art of Assyria never aimed at showing the nobler features of life.

GREECE AND ROME

Unlike the artists in Egypt and Assyria those in Greece had much more freedom. They were not bound to traditional ways and could choose subjects which attracted or pleased them. The victory in the Persian wars let loose a great deal of creative energy. The destruction of parts of Athens gave the Athenians the opportunity to rebuild and ambitious schemes were put forward. The Parthenon is probably the greatest of the buildings in this programme of reconstruction, and the work of Myron the sculptor reached a perfection never matched in Roman times.

Notice how, in ideas on government and in the arts, we return again and again to the fifth century B.C. in Greece. This is

An Assyrian winged bull

◀ *A Greek actor*

A discus thrower ▶

A Greek pitcher

◀ *A Mosaic–Dionysus on a panther*

one of the most highly civilised periods in human history, only rivalled later by the Italian Renaissance and eighteenth century France.

Roman art owes much to Greek influence, and this has led many people to describe much of what the Romans produced as poor copies of Greek masterpieces. The Romans were not like the Greeks in outlook, they put more emphasis on efficiency, order and discipline rather than individuality. Consequently the Romans' greatest achievements were in architecture rather than in sculpture and painting. In a later volume we shall

deal with the outstanding engineers of Queen Victoria's reign and consider the orderly beauty created by I. K. Brunel on the Great Western Railway. A similar beauty is to be found in many of the masterpieces built by Roman architects and engineers.

The Norman Conquest was followed by a period of remarkably good building, centred around the construction and decoration of churches. Before the Conquest Anglo-Saxon achievement had been more in the field of jewellery, metal work and the making of manuscripts.

144

The Porta Maggiore, Rome ▲
A page from the Lindisfarne Gospels ▼

The outlook of the medieval artist is shown in the following passage from a manual written by an artistic monk for the instruction of his pupils. He wrote:

"In illuminating the vaults and the walls with every diversity of handiwork, and all the lines of the rainbow, thou hast in a manner shown forth to every beholder a vision of God's paradise, bright as springtide with flowers of every hue, and with the fresh green of grass and leaves . . . whereby thou makest men to praise God in creatures, and to preach His wonders in His works. For the beholder's eye knoweth not where first to rest its gaze; if we look upward to the vaults, they are even as a mantle embroidered with flowers; if, again, we look upon the walls, there also is a kind of paradise; or if we consider the light that streams through the window, then we cannot but marvel at the priceless beauty of the glass and at the variety of this most precious work. . . ."

The Arts

THE MIDDLE AGES

Medieval art, like that of Egypt, was a group effort. One can picture the scene in a village, near to which a church was being constructed. Everyone would be interested in the work of the masons, carpenters and other craftsmen. The church under construction, or completed, would be at the centre of life and these illustrations give some indication of the achievement of medieval craftsmen.

Stained glass window, Eaton Bishop ▶

Interior, Wells Cathedral ▼

The Font in Lenton Church ▼

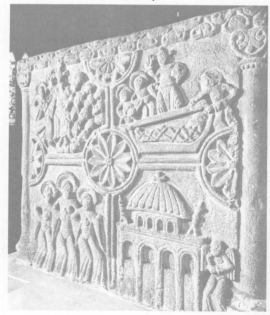

The Cloisters, Salisbury Cathedral ▲

The nave roof, Woolpit Church ▼

North transept wall, Hexham Priory ▼

MUSICAL INSTRUMENTS

Early man made use of his voice, the hard ground and stone in his music making. Music played, and still does play, an important part in man's moments of greatest happiness or despair, whether marriage was being celebrated or a loved one being mourned.

The instruments used by the people of Stone Ages and the Ancient World are dealt with together in six main groups which you will see illustrated in the following pages.

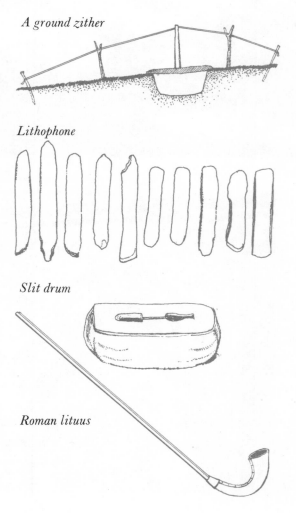

A ground zither

Lithophone

Slit drum

Roman lituus

The use of percussion instruments is always associated with primitive peoples, and it is not unusual for some to regard drumming as mere physical exercise. The drumming techniques of many Africans to-day are much more developed and subtle than the dull beat which has become part of so much Western popular music, and it is worth noting that many jazz musicians turn to the rhythms of Latin American and African folk music when they run out of ideas.

Some stone carvings show ancient Assyrians beating their throats. Similarly, in modern Africa the voice is used purely as an instrument, not merely for producing speech or song. Clapping the hands, slapping the thighs, or stamping on the hard ground are still effective parts of primitive percussion, but rattles, scrapers and clappers can add to the variety of sound.

The sistrum, a rattle, was used in Ancient Egypt, Rome and elsewhere. Scrapers were often made of bone and were believed to have certain magical qualities. The playing of bone scrapers made from previous kills played an important part in hunting rituals.

In Africa the earth was used in the construction of the ground zither, the central part was placed on a stone slab over what we would call an "echo chamber". The string of the zither was beaten with twigs. Slabs of stone of great antiquity which gave different notes were found in Indo-China in 1949 and they formed a crude but effective lithophone.

A wide range of drums was used in early times, some examples are the slit drum and the gourd drum. It was during the Dark Ages that the kettledrum, important in the modern orchestra, made its appearance in Europe. It was brought by the Arabs who conquered part of Europe and much of North Africa.

In the opinion of at least one expert the musical bow was in use as early as 15 000 B.C., the approximate date of a French cave painting showing a bow being put to such use. Ground bows are used in parts of Africa to-day. Other stringed instruments used were zithers, harps, lyres and lutes. The illustration of Egyptian musicians shows a harp, lute and double-pipe being played.

For over thirty centuries the harp was the most common musical instrument of Mesopotamia, and Egypt, whereas in

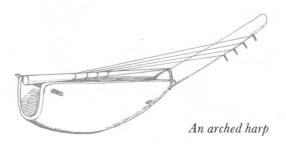

An arched harp

Egyptian musicians

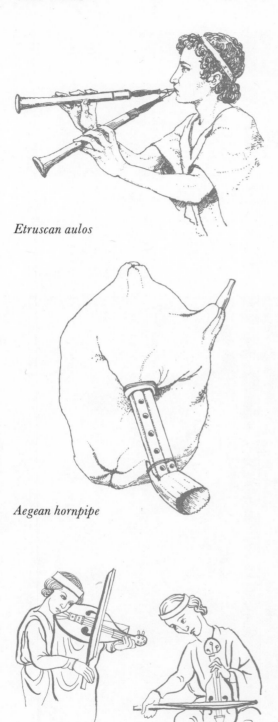

Etruscan aulos

Aegean hornpipe

13th century fiddles

Ancient Greece the lyre was the national instrument. The lute was used in Mesopotamia as early as 2000 B.C. but it took a long time before it became a popular instrument.

One of the greatest mysteries is the origin of the fiddle which cannot be dated before the ninth century A.D. The illustration shows thirteenth century fiddles which were similar to lutes in shape.

The flute and pipe were used in Ancient Egypt, Mesopotamia and Greece. These took a variety of forms from double pipes to bagpipes and panpipes. By Medieval times the pipe and tabor player was a one man band and in England provided the music for the Morris Dancers.

At the end of the Middle Ages the recorder had made its appearance and groups of recorder players performed in consort. The trumpets with their regal sound, and horns with their mellow sound had their parts to play in the Ancient World, one to provide a martial blast, the other to summon hunt or herd. You can hear recordings made recently with trumpets found in the tombs of Ancient Egypt, and an impressive sound they make too.

The history of brass instruments in Europe really begins in the Middle Ages, though the Roman litus and Danish lurs were brass instruments of a much earlier date.

Many of the buildings, pieces of sculpture and paintings produced in the Ancient civilisations are beautiful, but, with the exception of Ancient Greece, the artist copied from existing models. Later artists were more adventurous and expressed their own ideas.

Government

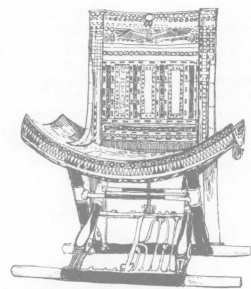

An Egyptian throne

Earliest man, so far as we know, did not live in isolated families, but in bands. They were social beings living together, working together for mutual benefit and facing common dangers. A gang of children can organise many enjoyable games together and on occasions can do good turns for the people in their neighbourhood. On the other hand they can spend their time causing a great deal of nuisance and damage. In the same way, people living together as a nation, or even nations living amongst other nations, can either live peacefully and usefully, or fight and squabble. It is the job of a government to try to provide the right conditions for people to live together happily. Whether we learn to do this or not depends upon the ideas and beliefs we share together.

There is great economy in working together, for instance in 1935 one American farming family could produce enough to feed nine city families. The surpluses that farmers produce feed the remainder of the population and give them the opportunity to do a vast number of other jobs. In Ancient Egypt and the other river civilisations farmers produced a surplus which was used to support other specialist workers. The government could increase output by organising an efficient system of canals and embankments in places such as the Nile Valley.

The government may often use force to make sure that all citizens carry out their duties. Sometimes governments have misused force. This is one of the dangers of allowing some parts of one's life to be organised by a government. But we must remember that social progress like technical progress brings with it greater responsibilities. The dangers of atomic warfare are clear to everybody, but the dangers of bad government are more difficult to appreciate.

The beliefs of the community, especially those dealing with behaviour towards one another and the rights of property owners, were set down in laws. One of the most famous early codes of law was that of Hammurabi, ruler of Babylon (2123–2081 B.C.). The beginning of his code tells of his aims. They were "to uphold justice in the land, to banish the proud and the oppres-

Government

sor, that the great shall not despoil the weak. . . ." Most of the 282 clauses in his code seem good common sense and include the punishment of officials for neglect of duty, penalties for people who steal or who fail to maintain their part of the irrigation system, provision for compensation for damages and penalties for assault. Some punishments seem harsh to-day, for instance keepers of beershops who charged too much were to be drowned in beer and surgeons who caused a patient's death were to lose their hands.

Amenophis IV

The people in Ancient Egypt or Sumer had no say in government. They provided the labour for the patient build-up of civilisation, and later the labour to serve the war aims of tyrants. By the time the Assyrians gained control over the Near East the king was no longer a helpful law giver, but a tyrant who massacred whole populations, took others as slaves and offered nothing constructive to those he ruled. The blood-stained Assyrian empire was followed by the Persian empire which was far better, and from which Alexander and the Romans learnt how to rule a vast empire through one man.

THE GREEK CITY STATE

The Acropolis: Athens

The Greeks were not united into one country until they were conquered by Philip of Macedon. Before this time they lived in city states. A city state such as Athens contained about 300 000 people who were divided into three main classes, the slaves, the resident foreigners or metics, and the citizens. Only the citizens played an active part in the government of the city. Juries were elected and the various districts of Athens elected candidates for the central government of the city. The Council of Five Hundred was the central governing body and since this was rather a large number, decisions were made, with the consent of the council, by a committee of fifty of the councilmen. Most citizens would serve on one of the governing bodies and this type of government where the people play a part is called democratic.

The Greeks believed that the city state existed to bring about the good life and this idea, along with the use of elected representatives who discussed, framed and executed policy, are two priceless gifts to mankind by these talented people. Pericles was one of the greatest statesmen who served Athens and when he spoke in honour of the many Athenian soldiers who had fallen in battle he reminded his fellow citizens of the greatness of Athens. He said:

"In magnifying the city I have magnified them. For what treasure can the thoughtful man prefer to that? What possession has he which he can hold in higher esteem or for which he will risk and sacrifice more? Shall he prefer his property or his family? Of what use is property except to enable a man to enjoy that higher good which comes from having an active share in the city's life? And of what value is family, even though it be of ancient and honourable lineage, except as it gives one an entrance into that higher form of social relationship represented by civil life? Above all faction, above all lesser groups of any sort, stands the city, which gives to all of them their meaning and their value."

Unlike the tyrannies of the Ancient World the city state such as Athens allowed each citizen to contribute to the community according to his own ability. We too try to see that each individual is able to play his part in the life of the country.

THE ROMAN EMPIRE

The Romans were practical and never reached the artistic heights of the Greeks, but in the matter of government it is often the practical people who are most successful. The Romans found ways of governing a large empire successfully and many of the best ideas of the Greeks and the Romans were embodied in Roman law. This body of law survived in the Byzantine Empire and was studied in the Middle Ages and finally transmitted down to modern times. As the Emperor Justinian states at the beginning of the Institutes, a manual for law students in the Byzantine Empire:

"The Imperial Majesty should be armed with laws as well as glorified with arms, that there may be good government in times of both war and peace. . . ."

A Tribune

The barbarian peoples were by no means as highly organised or civilised as the Romans or the Greeks. The Icelandic sagas and the laws of the Vikings show a primitive and brutal community. But there is a strong individualism about the heroes, which was one of the best qualities of these people. It is possibly this quality of common sense and self reliance, which lingered on in their descendants in Normandy and which in turn through Duke William was brought to England, that made England an orderly, powerful monarchy by the twelfth century.

THE GOVERNMENT AND THE LAW IN ENGLAND, 1066–1422

As William I extended his conquest of England he divided the land amongst his barons. They were given scattered possessions and were responsible for good order and the management of these estates. His laws, especially the forest laws, were harsh and despite the order and efficiency of William's government it is clear that he and his nobles had the privileges, whilst the bulk of Englishmen carried out the duties. Henry II is very important for he was successful in making sure that the King's Laws were carried out in all parts of his kingdom. He sent his own judges to all the shires of England to enforce his law and to this day judges still go to the assizes to carry out the law.

An ordeal

Before Henry's reign (1154–89) trial by ordeal was often used. The accused had to put his forearm into hot water, or carry a heavy piece of hot iron a few paces. The scalded or burned limb was bound up and examined later. If it was inflamed it was a sign of guilt, if it was healing up it was a sign of innocence. These methods were replaced by a jury system. The juries were the forerunners of present day juries, although their work was not the same.

Henry was a strong king and made sure that his laws were carried out. Castles which had been built without a royal licence in previous reigns were destroyed. Only in his struggle with the church was Henry unsuccessful.

Henry II's achievement is a reminder that the success of good laws is in the hands of those who carry them out. It is no use having a good set of rules if a lot of people disobey them, and never suffer for their actions. Often when a new country is created its rulers draw up a very good set of laws, but find great difficulty in getting them carried out. In England laws have been passed one after the other throughout the centuries and the method of lawmaking has gradually become a tradition.

The early Norman kings had a council made up of barons and religious leaders, but in the thirteenth century the first parliaments were held. In 1265 Henry III summoned not only barons, bishops and abbots, but two knights from each shire and two citizens from certain towns. Kings, such as Edward I, continued to call parliaments because they were useful as a means of getting the people to accept fresh taxes, and as a channel through which the people could air their grievances. People more readily accepted taxes if they were consulted in advance, and they were less likely to rebel if given an opportunity to complain.

It is important to see that Parliament was very different in the thirteenth century from present day and we shall trace its development in further volumes. Decisions such as Edward I's promise in 1297 not to levy taxes without consent, and Parliament's approval of the deposition of Edward II are an indication of the part which Parliament began to play in the nation's affairs.

Ideas

Ammon-Re—the Egyptian sun god

One of the greatest differences between men and animals is that men's actions spring more from ideas, and animals' from instincts.

Earliest man had little time to think for he was busy keeping body and soul together, even so he had to use his wits or perish. He was so much weaker than the forces of nature around him that he had to out-think them. He learned to observe the habits of animals and the nature of his surroundings, just as we do in science. He chose to live in groups for safety and then had to think how the tribe should be governed. We call these studies politics and law. He pondered on the meaning of life and tried to explain its mysteries, and so religion and philosophy were born. He lived in the great unknown and the man who had even a little knowledge was respected; the magician of the tribe was scientist, doctor, lawyer, priest and philosopher rolled into one.

EGYPT

The civilisation of the Nile lasted for nearly 4000 years, so its ideas must have been workable, or it would have crumbled away much sooner. The people of Egypt were farmers who depended upon the sun and the Nile; those sources of life were worshipped as gods, for example the sun god was Ammon-Re. When people think that the forces of nature are gods we call their religion Pantheism, after the Greek god who was half man and half goat.

The difficulty with thinking is that words are often inadequate to express thoughts, and in religion early men, like children, tried to tell a truth in story form. The flooding of the Nile each year was said to be the goddess Isis weeping for the lost Osiris; we can see this method of picture words in the book of Genesis. The governors of the people found it useful to encourage the idea that their rulers were gods. The Pharaohs did this and so did the Caesars of Rome. Most religions contain the idea of life after death. The

155

Egyptians were very concerned with the idea of "heaven"; this is why the wealthy built pyramids and tombs and why they preserved their bodies as mummies so that they could be used again. They even put food and trinkets in their coffins to help them on the journey between life and death.

Religious ideas were hard to separate from what we would call science. Egyptian priests were astronomers, men who study the sky and the planets, and also astrologers, men who use astronomy to foretell the future. They plotted the courses of the stars and used mathematics to calculate angles and distances. The building of the pyramids also needed mathematics, but as yet mathematics was practical rather than theoretical; it was useful more than thoughtful.

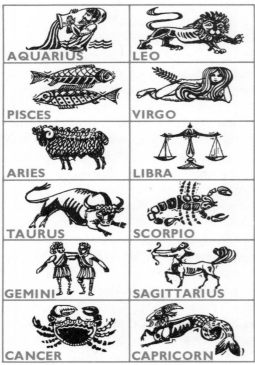

Astrological symbols

THE GREEKS

The Greeks passed on many great ideas which are part of our way of life to-day. They did not have much to offer in religious ideas however, for they still thought of gods as spirits of nature. The Greek and Roman families of gods are the same, only their names are different. The Greek father of the gods was Zeus, the Roman was Jupiter.

Greek mythology is still read, and the stories of Heracles, Aphrodite and Poseidon are well known. The Greeks feared their gods for they did not think of them as being good, but angry and spiteful and very likely to take their revenge on mere mortals unless they were pleased. Socrates, one of the great philosophers, was forced to drink hemlock and kill himself. Because he denied the gods he was blamed for the troubles then facing Athens.

Greek words such as atoms, physics and Archimedes are common in your science lessons. Modern science can be dated from Thales of Miletus (*c.* 7 B.C.) who thought that water was the prime element; later Greeks thought there were four—earth, fire, air and water. Although we now know this to be untrue it provided chemistry with the beginning of its table of elements.

Aristotle (384–322 B.C.) tried to think scientifically and discover "laws of nature"; he used scientific methods of observation and experiment. He tried to discover the nature of things (scientists call this the structure of matter), and the nature of moving objects, such as the movement of the earth. Many of his ideas were proved wrong, but his method of working and thinking is the start of true scientific method.

Hippocrates (460–357 B.C.) did the

Socrates

same for medicine by studying the human body and trying to explain scientifically the cause of disease instead of blaming magic. Doctors to-day take a Hippocratic Oath, promising to follow their profession faithfully.

Thinkers might have theories about the nature of things, but there were some who experimented in order to change one substance into another. In particular they hoped to change an ordinary metal like lead into a precious one like gold; these men were called Alchemists. About 200 B.C. a Greek living in Alexandria called Bolos wrote up the work of the Alchemists in a book called "Physika".

You can see how the borderline between science and magic was still shadowy; this was also true of Astronomy and Astrology. Much later about A.D. 200 another Greek, called Ptolemy who lived in Alexandria summarised Greek Astronomy in a scientific way. Meanwhile the astrologer plied his wares as a sort of court magician.

Alexandria was the place where Greek and Egyptian thinking met, and perhaps the Greek you know best, Euclid (300 B.C.) lived there too. He brought together many of the Greek ideas on geometry, and you may have started to learn some of his theorems. The Greeks liked mathematics,

and Plato, better known as a philosopher, is said to have written over his Academy, "Let no one ignorant of geometry enter here."

The greatest Greek thinkers were called Philosophers. They were not as interested in subjects as in learning as a whole. They wrestled with the meaning of life, the universe and men. Plato, Socrates and Aristotle are the best known, their teachings on the nature of men and their institutions are true in any age. Many of our ideas on truth, beauty and virtue stem from Ancient Greece, and even our form of government, democracy, owes its origin to the little city states.

THE ROMANS

The Romans were not great original thinkers, they chose to copy and improve other people's ideas. Men like Galen (A.D. 130–201) continued the search for medical knowledge, but by and large the Romans were more concerned with building roads and aqueducts than playing with ideas.

They did add to men's ideas on Law, which is not surprising for they had to govern a large Empire and law deals with the way people behave in their community, or state. Roman law insisted on the importance of the state and demanded absolute obedience to it. This idea of the all-powerful state appears time and time again in history and in this century Germany and Italy have suffered because of it. Rome sheltered Greek ideas and when Rome fell, these ideas fell too; they lay buried for centuries and only gradually re-appeared.

THE HEBREWS

Through the Roman Empire also flowed the other stream of our thinking, the religious ideas of the Jews. The Jewish

*The Testimonia document
from the Dead Sea Scrolls*

scriptures are part of our Bible, we call them the old Testament. These contain the history of how God showed himself to men through his chosen people, the Israelites. This God, Yahweh, was not an image nor were there many gods, there was only one. He was still feared, but he was not mean and petty. He was good and just. The Jews believed, and still do, that a Messiah or Saviour will come to unite the Good God and Sinful Man.

CHRISTIANITY

Christianity developed from the Jewish faith, for Jesus was a Jew and Christians believe that he was the Messiah. Jesus was condemned by the leaders of his own people because he claimed to be "the Son of God", that is, that he was God in human form. This idea is a great chal-

lenge, for it means that the invisible God has broken through into history as a humble carpenter. Jesus' perfect life tells us that God is love, his loving death underlines this, and his rising from the dead promises life after death.

Jesus taught for only three short years in an out of the way part of a great Empire, yet his life has affected the whole of our history; we even date our history from his birth, Anno Domini. Jesus' teachings have always linked up with politics and his insistence that individual people are important whatever their colour or creed because all are children of God has been woven into our life. Like most great ideas, men have fallen short of them in the last 2000 years.

THE DARK AGES
AND MIDDLE AGES

The Dark Ages were not as black as they were once painted, but they lacked the ideas of the Ancient World. Christianity managed to keep the torch of learning flickering in its monasteries. Religious thinkers like St. Augustine of Hippo in his "City of God" and St. Thomas Aquinas in his "Summa Theologica" tried to combine Greek Philosophy and Christian teaching. Aquinas gave a Christian interpretation of the pagan idea that rulers were gods, by the idea that rulers were appointed by God to rule provided they ruled for the benefit of all and according to God's guidance.

In the Middle Ages there were no nations as we know them; there was no Germany or France for example, and thinking was quite different from that of to-day. There was an international religion, Catholicism, an international language, Latin, and the hope of an international state, the Holy Roman Empire. Our age also thinks internationally and hopes for international government of some kind in the work of the United Nations Organisation.

Organisations usually have two faces, one is stern and looks back, one is hopeful and looks forward. The stern face of the Church in the Middle Ages was the Inquisition, which tried to stamp out new thoughts and labelled them as heresies. It used the methods of its own day, torture and execution, but like others since it made the mistake of thinking that ideas can be stifled by fear. The other side of its face is seen in forward-looking priests like John Ball, the priest of the Peasants' Revolt, whose doggerel:

"When Adam delved and Eve span
Who was then a gentleman?"

was a very dangerous question in 1381. Another, John Wycliffe, opened up a whole new field of thinking by translating the Bible into English. Great ideas were afoot by the fifteenth century, and were galloping by the sixteenth.

ISLAM

The spur to this new thinking came from outside Europe proper. In the seventh century A.D. the prophet Mohammed taught in Arabia; his Holy Writ, the Koran, preached that Allah was the one God, that Jesus had been merely another prophet. The way to heaven was by following a strict code of behaviour and ceremonies, and in this it is more like the Jewish faith than Christianity. During the seventh century Mohammedanism moved into the Mediterranean world. It spread into Spain and Sicily and even to the gates of Vienna. It became a vast state called Islam. It came into contact with the old learning of Greece, Egypt and even India at a time when the barbarians were ignoring it in Europe.

An alchemist

Our word "algebra" is an Arabic word, and our numbers 0, 1, 2, 3, etc. are Arabic. Can you imagine how hard it would be to multiply if we had kept to the old Roman numbers, e.g. xv × x = cl? Greek mathematics were eagerly translated by the Arab scholars and studied in universities, three hundred years before our so called "older universities", Oxford and Cambridge, were founded.

There was a renewed interest in alchemy. Some enquiries, such as the search for the elixir (an Arab word) of life, or the Philosopher's Stone which would change the nature of substances, were fruitless. Others, more useful, were in fact a renewal of the search for knowledge in the manner of the Greeks.

Men thought. They were eager for learning and their ideas beat against the walls of Europe, breached them and poured into its lands, at first as a trickle but eventually as a flood. By the fifteenth century the Renaissance or re-birth of learning had begun. Modern times were on the way.

159

INDEX